N A M E

T H A T

C A T

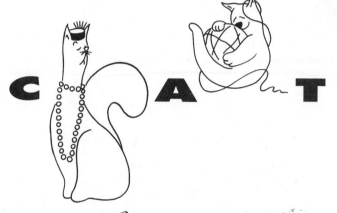

Over 1,000
Inventive and Colorful Names

DOUG CASSIDY

CROWN PUBLISHERS, INC.
NEW YORK

Produced by Alison Brown Cerier Book Development, Inc.

Published by Crown Publishers, Inc., 201 East 50th Street, New York, New York
10022. Member of the Crown Publishing Group.

CROWN is a trademark of Crown Publishers, Inc.

Manufactured in the United States of America

Illustrations by Jeff Erickson

Library of Congress Cataloging-in-Publication Data

Cassidy, Doug.
    Name that cat: over 1,000 inventive and colorful names / by Doug Cassidy. —
1st ed.
    1. Cats—Names. I. Title.
    SF442.4.C37 1992
    636.8'0887—dc20   91-38393
                                               CIP

ISBN 0-517-58521-9

10 9 8 7 6 5 4 3 2 1

First Edition

For Susan

Special thanks to Jane Meara, my lifelong friend, and now editor, who always believed; to book developer Alison Brown Cerier, who from start to finish was always there to help; to the Southampton Library Staff for all their assistance; to the Cat Fanciers' Association, Inc., for their kindness in helping with this project; and to Herbert and Mary Boehl for all their support.

CONTENTS

N A M E

T H A T

C A T

THE NAMING OF CATS

Finding the right name for your cat can be a tricky business. It's different than naming a child. There you can fudge (which is a pretty good name for a cat) a bit by naming a girl after Aunt Ellen or a boy after Uncle Albert. Or you can name a son after his father and everyone will quickly agree that it's a wonderful choice. Not so for a cat. There are very few Bobo Juniors around the neighborhood.

Naming a cat is a different matter altogether. When it comes to naming your cat, you're free to be imaginative. There are so many variables and possibilities: Color or combination of colors, appearance, personality, and temperament traits all suggest potential names. Living people, dead people, sports heroes, mythical creatures, and legendary characters are sources, too. *Name That Cat* will help you to winnow these choices down to just the right one for your kitty.

First, some general rules to help you in your search. Rule Number One: Remember that the name you choose will say as much about you as it does about your cat. It will immediately be clear how you personally view this human/cat relationship. Please don't start off on the wrong foot. Make a note right now—negative names are out. Names like Eight Ball and Dingbat are not for us. You love your cat, your cat loves you. Pick a positive name. Rule Number Two: Make your name search fun. Avoid family fights. Don't argue. Have a good time.

1

Naming is one of the great parts of loving a cat. Be silly. Let you imagination run free. Think of the things that characterize your cat, then go ahead and pick the name that fits. Rule Number Three: You'll know your cat's name when you find it. There'll be no need to go any farther. She really is _____!

REAL CHARACTERS

All cats are characters. Some are sweethearts, some tough guys, some clowns. Look deep inside your cat's being and choose a name that captures his true personality. Is your cat a Spike or Sweetpea, a Bubbles or a Boomerang?

August. *M/F.* For the dignified or grand cat.

Beamer. *M/F.* For those who love their BMWs. You know who I mean.

Beans. *M/F.* For Mexican jumping beans—the ones that wiggle and roll and bounce all over the place just like a kitten at play.

Bingo. *M/F.* You've hit the jackpot with a cat named Bingo.

Blarney. *M/F.* The Irish cat who gets what he wants through soft-soaping and flummery. He's a flatterer, but don't you love that Blarney?

Blue. *M/F.* Short for "true blue," for the cat who's right there with you through thick and thin. An obvious name for a Russian Blue, too.

Boomerang. *M/F.* Boomer for short. For the cat who just keeps coming back for more.

Boycott. *M/F.* A cat named Boycott refuses to participate in any activity that doesn't suit his fancy, especially eating his dinner.

Broadway. *M/F.* A cat named Broadway thinks he is a star.

Bubbles. *M/F.* The effervescent kitten with boundless enthusiasm.

Caddie. *M/F.* Cats don't make good caddies, but they do enjoy playing with golf balls.

Chase. *M/F.* For the rather stuffy cat in pinstripes who controls the money. These days, it's nice to have a banker on your side.

Checkmate. *M/F.* This cat, as opposed to cousin Stalemate, plays to win.

Choo Choo. *M/F.* When this kitten gets rolling, it takes a lot of track to slow her down.

Chuckles. *M/F.* A cat named Chuckles is the family clown.

Contac. *M/F.* The name of this cold remedy is an abbreviation for "continuous action."

Cosmos. *M/F.* Cosmos is the cat who views things on a grand scale.

Crackerjack. *M/F.* This kitten is named for the caramel-covered popcorn with a prize in every box. The word is slang for "top" or "best"—just like your kitty.

Deuces. *M/F.* The deuce cat tends to draw low in life. But in finding his new home, he finally pulled an ace.

Doctor. *M/F.* The cat who makes you feel better, no matter how low you're feeling or how sick you may be.

Dot. *F.* For the cat with the spotty disposition.

Fax. *M/F.* Some cats have to have everything yesterday.

Francis Xavier Cat. *M.* Born of Irish stock in the Bronx, FX has been in a scrape or two, but he worked his way out of the alley and, like most of his friends, is sitting pretty now.

Gimp. *M.* Short for Tony the Gimp, this is the cat with underworld connections. Forget asking how Tony got the bad leg—you don't really want to know.

Goblin. *M/F.* Goblins are not-overly-attractive sprites who are usually up to no good. A cat named Goblin has a mischievous and sometimes malicious streak.

Grapes. *M/F.* This kitten's disposition is on the sour side, and he's the first to complain.

Half Hitch. *M/F.* Named after the traditional sailor's knot, Half Hitch is good luck on board.

Happy. *M/F.* Usually a name given by a child and perfectly appropriate—cats are happy and they make us happy, too.

Hiss. *M/F.* Hiss is an appropriate if unpleasant name for a not-so-nice cat.

Hype. *M/F.* The kitten with the tendency to exaggerate. He runs too fast, meows too loudly, eats too quickly, and jumps much too high.

JD. *M/F.* Back in the good old days, kids who broke the law were called juvenile delinquents or JDs. The police issued JD cards; you had to be pretty bad to get one. A kitten named JD should wear his card on his collar for all to see.

Kindles. *M/F.* Kindles is the kitten who lights a match under everyone in your household. By the way, a group of kittens is called a "kindle."

Kitten Catchatorre. *M/F.* A play on chicken cacciatore, an Italian chicken dish with wine and mushrooms.

Kitten Emeritus. *M/F.* This cat is now retired from active duty as the number-one disturber of the peace. But the behavior of Kitten Emeritus during the formative months was so bad that it will always be remembered with awe.

Knucks. *M/F.* Knucks, short for Knuckles, earned his reputation in back-alley fisticuffs.

Leather. *M/F.* Some cats like leather. Then again, some cats are *like* leather—as tough as a U.S. Marine.

Legs. *M/F.* For the dancer, split end, or gangster in your family.

Lionel. *M.* Named for the train set of your youth. Like your cat, it brought hours of fun.

Lotto. *M/F.* Worth a million, maybe more. It takes only one Lotto to make you the big winner.

Lucky. *M/F.* Could be named for the infamous gangster, Lucky Luciano, but much better for the cat who has everything, including a nice, safe home.

Lulu. *F.* This cat's a lulu—wonderful, marvelous, just plain great.

Madam. *F.* For the grande dame of the household. Impervious to criticism, Madam will do as she pleases.

Miss Minion. *F.* Miss Minion is the spoiled or highly favored family pet.

Mister Softee. *M.* For the cat who's a real pushover.

Mistletoe. *M/F.* This cat loves to collect kisses. Nice for the cat who came into your life around the Christmas holidays.

Mogul. *M/F.* Big shot, big wheel, important cat with big fish to fry, that's the cat named Mogul. Unfortunately, it seems he's become too big to spend much time with his family.

More. *M/F.* Enough is never enough for this kitten when it comes to food, play, or mischief.

Moxie. *M/F.* A cat named Moxie has pluck. "Moxie" means the ability to face difficulty with courage.

MP. *M/F.* MP is the cat who acts like a military policeman. Just try to have a little fun, and you can bet that MP will race in to break it up.

Mumbles. *M/F.* Mumbles always has something to say but never quite comes out with a clear meow, or yowl, or even purr.

Negatory. *M/F.* This cat's name is taken from trucker CB radio slang for "no." Negatory is the cat who always says no—to everything, on principle.

Old Chum. *M/F.* Old Chum is your partner, intimate, friend, playmate, and alter ego. This cat knows you inside and out and is still your best friend. What could be better than that?

PC. *M/F.* PC is short for personal computer. This high-tech cat loves using the mouse to give commands.

Penny. *F.* A Penny saved from an animal shelter will pay dividends forever.

Perpetrator. *M/F.* Perp for short. Although the police generally use the phrase "alleged perpetrator" in deference to our legal system, there's never a doubt—you know your cat did it.

Pickles. *M/F.* No matter how you slice it, this name was made for the cat who's a real dilly.

Pierre. *M*. This Parisian cat is much too smooth and continental to be called Pete. He's trés fond of natural gourmet cat food.

Pip. *M/F*. This cat's a Pip, a real ace.

Plucky. *M/F*. Plucky is a brave little kitten who, even though he has a thin and scrawny body, has the heart and fighting spirit of a lion.

Polo. *M/F*. For the cat who's fond of games played on horseback. If the truth be known, it's the clothes that catch this cat's eye.

Preacher. *M/F*. The cat who can rain down old-fashioned fire and brimstone on any tomfoolery with just a look. There was a powerful Brooklyn Dodgers pitcher named Preacher Roe.

Prof. *M/F*. Sometimes the Professor flaunts her knowledge, but usually she just keeps to herself, quietly thinking greater thoughts than we students can imagine.

Pug. *M*. This name is usually given to dogs, but some cats simply won't be denied. If your cat looks like a fighter, walks like a fighter, and talks like a fighter, then go ahead and make his day by choosing this name.

Rickshaw Bob. *M*. Rickshaw Bob is the kind of cat who always operates on the fringe. A transplanted American, he's in on everything. But, unfortunately, most of what he's in on is trouble.

Ripley. *M/F*. Ripley is the "believe it or not" cat. Strange but true.

Rolaids. *M/F.* Rolaids spells relief for you. All she has to do is jump into your lap to make you smile.

Rooster. *M.* A fun name for a male cat. You know the type—struts around like he owns the house. Even the tail is sort of, well, braggadocio.

Rosie. *F.* Everything's coming up roses when this kitten's around. Rosie's cheerfulness puts a glow in your cheeks.

Rx. *M/F.* Rx is the prescription cat, guaranteed to cure what ails you.

Sandman. *M.* Sandman is the sleepyhead cat. After dinner he can hardly stifle a yawn before it's off to bed for a sound night's sleep. Cats named Sandman are the ideal pets for people who like to spend long hours happily curled up with a good book.

Sarge. *M/F.* This cat is in charge. Forget the officers—we all know who makes things run.

Silk Sock Sam. *M.* Silk Sock Sam is a dandy. He's a sharp dresser and a cat about town. This cat's a ladies' man and he'll try to get out each night to prove it.

Slick. *M.* The cat who's too smart and smooth for his own good.

Snake. *M/F.* This swivel-hipped cat's name is guaranteed to raise a few eyebrows.

Sparkplug. *M/F.* Also known as Sparky, this cat gives you a charge.

Spike. *M.* If you see this cat coming, better step aside. He's the original West Side tom and he's as tough as nails.

Stitch. *M/F.* For the cat whose antics keep you in stitches—or for the cat whose ill temper *puts* you in stitches.

Subway. *M/F.* Named for the underground train system, this cat loves to be under beds, chairs, shelves. . . .

Sunshine. *M/F.* Sunshine comes softly through not only your window, but almost everything else as well. A cheery disposition gives this kitten her name.

Sweetpea. *F.* April's flower represents innocence. Maybe your kitten isn't exactly innocent, and knocking over a vase is as close as she ever comes to flowers. But she is small, cute, and really very sweet.

Tango. *M/F.* For the dancing cat with the Latin flair.

Tiffany. *F.* Tiffany is the upscale kitten with style. She's a pampered cat and proud of it. Like the jewelry store, she's first class all the way.

Tom. *M.* A generic name for a male cat. Baby boomers may call this cat Tommy after the rock opera by the Who.

Twister. *M/F.* Like the game that requires participants to place their hands and feet on different colored dots, kittens named Twister cause entanglement and confusion.

Verboten. *M/F.* Whatever is off-limits attracts the cat named Verboten, from the German word for "forbidden." This cat tests every rule in the house.

Vidalia. *M/F.* Named after the Georgia onions so sweet that some people eat them like apples. A cat named Vidalia has a disposition to match.

Waiter. *M.* You can call this cat Waiter or anything you want—you'll never get his attention anyway.

Walter Mitty. *M.* In this kitten's daydreams, he's a lion taking on the neighborhood pit bull.

Xerox. *M/F.* The gold standard in copycats.

Yale. *M/F.* For the bright kitten who likes to play in the ivy.

ENTERTAINING CATS

If your cat is always the star of the show, consider a name from the movies, television, theater, popular music, or the comic pages. Bogie and Pooh Bah, Satchmo and Schmoo—that's entertainment!

Addams. *M.* Charles Addams, *The New Yorker* magazine cartoonist who created the Addams family, loved animals. A cat named Addams will only be happy with an eccentric family.

Bilco. *M.* There's more than a little Sergeant Bilco in most cats. Bilco, played by Phil Silvers, had a scheme for everything. But when he orders, "Look alive, Doberman," cats stand up and cheer.

Bing. *M.* Like Bing Crosby, this cat is a crooner with style. His purr is like a melody.

Bogie. *M.* Like the characters played by Humphrey Bogart, this cat is tough and cynical but does subscribe to a code of honor.

Bojangles. *M.* Named after Bill "Bojangles" Robinson, about whom Jerry Jeff Walker wrote the song "Mr. Bojangles." A kitten with this name is fond of dogs, is light on his feet, and likes to dance the old soft shoe.

Boston Blackie. *M.* A reformed crook who helps solve crimes, Boston Blackie was a popular second-feature movie character. Cats named Boston Blackie are, at best, only partially reformed.

Bugs. *M.* What's up, Doc? Like the cartoon character Bugs Bunny, this kitten has a wise-guy attitude, and big ears as well.

Calypso. *M/F.* This kitten is always off exploring, like Jacques Cousteau's ship.

Captain Hooks. *M/F.* Captain Hook in *Peter Pan* had a hook instead of a hand. Blame this one on the crocodile. Captain Hooks the cat has multiple hooks on each paw and is more than ready to use them.

Captain Marvel. *M.* The world's mightiest mortal. In the comics, Captain Marvel was extremely hard on the bad guys. All bad-guy mice beware.

Captain Video. *M.* The radio and TV hero Captain Video was the guardian of the safety of the world. Lots of cats feel they are, too. The name can also be used for cats who love to watch TV.

Carlton. *M.* Named for Carlton the doorman from the TV series *Rhoda*. This cat has an uncanny ability to know when you're coming home. No matter what the time, he'll be waiting for you right by the front door.

Cat. *M/F.* Sometimes it seems as if one cat out of ten is named Cat. But if you'd like to say that your cat is named after a famous Cat, then how about the cat named Cat in *Breakfast at Tiffany's*?

Cat Ballou. *M.* In the movie of the same name, Lee Marvin starred as Cat Ballou, the washed-up old gunfighter. Real Cat Ballous may look a bit seedy and over the hill, but when the chips are down they'll be right there.

Chan. *M.* Short for Charlie Chan, the inveterate detective. Despite number-one son's constant interference, Chan is always two steps ahead of the criminal element.

Chester. *M.* The cat with a limp. On *Gunsmoke*, Chester, played by Dennis Weaver, is Marshal Matt Dillon's deputy. Just like this cat, he never let a little limp get him down.

Clark Kent. *M.* Like Clark Kent, he looks wimpy on the outside, but under all that fur beats the heart of Supercat.

Cosmic Creepers. *M/F.* The cat belonging to Angela Lansbury in the Walt Disney movie *Bedknobs and Broomsticks.*

Dancer. *M/F.* In addition to being the name of one of Santa's reindeer, Dancer is also the name of Walter Cronkite's cat.

Dolly. *F.* From the musical *Hello, Dolly.* This cat loves to make matches, and she's made a perfect one for herself with you.

Dr. Skat. *M/F.* Dr. Skat is one of author/singer Kinky Friedman's three cats. The other two are named Cuddles and Lady.

Dragon Lady. *F.* In the comic strip *Terry and the Pirates,* the Dragon Lady was very beautiful and very deadly. You certainly know a female feline who is a perfect fit for this one.

Duke. *M.* There once was a cat from a shelter who was the biggest, toughest hombre in the place. They called him Duke, for screen hero John Wayne.

Dylan. *M.* This cat's behavior is based on the rule "Don't Think Twice, It's Alright." For folksinger Bob Dylan.

E.T. *M/F.* The extraterrestrial cat. Like the character of the same name, E.T. is a little strange but wins everyone's hearts in the end.

Elmo. *M.* Elmo Lincoln, the first Tarzan. Your cat doesn't have to swing from vines to be considered a little wild around the house.

Elvis. *M.* For the heartthrob of a generation. Great for a cat with loose hips.

Elwood. *M.* In the movie *Harvey,* Elwood P. Dowd, played by Jimmy Stewart, is the friend of an invisible giant rabbit. Elwood's mother gives him some advice that everyone, including cats, should heed, "In this life, Elwood, you have to be very, very smart, or very, very pleasant. I recommend pleasant." For the nicest cat in your life.

Felix. *M.* The classic cartoon cat from the comics and motion pictures. Felix had a black body and white face and was guaranteed to make you laugh 'til your sides hurt.

Figaro. *M.* The cat in the carpenter's workshop in the Disney movie *Pinocchio.*

Flicks. *M/F.* He loves to watch old movies on TV.

Fonzi. *M.* Named after Arthur Fonzarelli, the high-school dropout played by Henry Winkler in TV's *Happy Days.* Like the Fonz, cats named Fonzi look tough and are tough but have hearts of gold.

Frank. *M.* Named after Francis Albert Sinatra, this cat does it his way. Also known as "Old Blue Eyes," the cat named Frank is a legend in his own time.

Friday. *M/F.* For the stoic cat whose refrain, like that of Sergeant Joe Friday on TV's *Dragnet,* is "Just the facts, ma'am." If you choose this name, you'll be able to greet your cat after a long week at work with "TGIF—Thank God It's Friday."

Fritz. *M*. Fritz the Cat, from the underground comic by Robert Crumb that was animated in 1972. Cats with this name are hippies at heart.

Garbo. *F*. Like actress Greta Garbo, this cat just wants to be alone.

Godot. *M/F*. If waiting for your cat to come home at night is becoming routine, name your kitten Godot. Then you'll be, as the play title says, *Waiting for Godot*.

Harry. *M*. For Harry Houdini and limited to those cats who have truly perfected the disappearing act.

Holly Golightly. *F*. Holly Golightly was the free spirit Audrey Hepburn played in *Breakfast at Tiffany's*. Actress Frances Farmer chose this name for her cat.

Iolanthe. *F*. From Gilbert and Sullivan's opera of the same name. Iolanthe was the "life and soul of fairyland," but she was banished for marrying a mortal. Thankfully, cats are more forgiving of each other when they take up residence with us mere mortals.

Isadora. *F*. This kitten believes in natural movement. Named for free-form dance pioneer Isadora Duncan, a cat named Isadora is likely to race across the room, bound over the couch, and pose briefly on the end table, all for the sake of art.

Jackie. *M/F.* Jackie the lion was named after Jacqueline Logan, star of the 1922 film *Burning Sands*. Noted for riding to the studio in a taxi and eating in the commissary with Cecil B. de Mille, Jackie was always regarded as the most human king of beasts. In all, Jackie appeared in over 250 pictures, including the classic *King of the Jungle* with Buster Crabbe.

Jazzman. *M.* The all-American entertainer cat. He's improvisational but loves to play in a group.

Joker. *M.* Usually a funnyman or a clown, this Joker is named after the sinister character played by Jack Nicholson in the movie *Batman*. Like the Cheshire Cat, it's his smile that gets you.

J.R. *M.* Like J. R. Ewing in *Dallas*, this kitten is a sneaky devil.

Kayo. *M/F.* In the cartoon strip *Gasoline Alley*, Kayo was Moon Mullins's son. He was a tough little kid. A cat named Kayo is pretty tough, too, and relies on a strong overhand paw to get the message across.

Kimble. *M.* Did you ever notice how some cats always seem to be running away from something or someone, almost as if they're fugitives? The real fugitive was Richard Kimble from the television series of the same name.

Kitty. *F.* *This* Kitty is named after the heart-of-gold Miss Kitty from the television show *Gunsmoke*.

Kojak. *M.* Who loves ya, baby? Kojak the cat, of course, named after Theo Kojak, the tough TV detective.

Your cat's perfect head of hair doesn't exclude the use of this name.

Lady Pepper. *F.* Pepper was the hero of a true rags-to-riches story. During the filming of a slapstick comedy, two bedraggled kittens wandered onto the stage. One ran away, but the other stayed on. Pepper was adopted and named by comedy king Mack Sennett and went on to be featured in many comedies, including *The Kitchen Lady,* starring Louise Fazenda.

Liebchen. *M/F.* From the movie *The Witches,* starring Angelica Huston. With a name meaning "dear little loved one," Liebchen belonged to the head witch.

Madonna. *F.* There's no need to justify this cat's love. Like the singer, a kitten named Madonna knows just what she's doing.

Mahout. *M/F.* A mahout is an elephant trainer. A cat named Mahout will train his family instead.

Mame. *F.* This name is from the play and movie *Auntie Mame.* Mame had a few years under her belt, but she really knew how to live. A good name for a cat with a free and open spirit.

Mandrake. *M.* For Mandrake the Magician of comic strip fame. This kitten may not pull rabbits out of hats, but he's sure to come up with a few surprises.

Marilyn. *F.* Some cats like it hot and this one, named after Marilyn Monroe, is one of them. Usually for the blonde kitten, but good for any aspiring to be bombshells.

Martha. *F.* For Martha Graham, one of the inventors of modern dance. A cat named Martha eschews the studied movement of other felines for a natural style charged with emotion and meaning.

Maynard. *M.* Maynard G. Krebs from *The Dobie Gillis Show* was an exceptionally kind beatnik. With the phrase "You rang?" Maynard always seemed to appear from out of nowhere.

McMurphy. *M.* In *One Flew Over the Cuckoo's Nest*, Randall Patrick McMurphy, played by Jack Nicholson, was the protagonist and "bull-goose looney" of the asylum.

Mikado. *M.* In Gilbert and Sullivan's comic opera, the Mikado is the emperor. Other names from the opera are the lovers Yum-Yum and Nanki-Poo, and Ko-Ko, the Lord High Executioner who isn't really suited for his job.

Ming. *M.* Less than a friend to Flash Gordon, Ming the Merciless never lets up. Kittens with this name show no mercy as disturbers of the peace.

Mister Rogers. *M.* Like his television counterpart, this cat is your children's favorite. He's soft and gentle and always has everyone's best interests in mind.

Morris. *M.* Morris is the orange cat famous for his television commercials. Morris is also one finicky eater.

Mr. Bluster. *M.* For the cat who is a little boastful and a little loud, like the character of the same name from *The Howdy Doody Show*. Your Mr. Bluster doesn't have to be the mayor of Doodyville to warrant this name.

Mugs McGinnis. *M.* The leader of the good-guy gang known as the Dead End Kids in the Bowery Boys films. Mugs is always in a scrape or a tiff with the law and he has trouble communicating, but his heart is in the right place.

Nathan. *M.* For Nathan Detroit, a gambler in *Guys and Dolls*. If, despite appearances, your cat has a good heart, this is the name for him.

Nijinsky. *M.* After the Russian ballet dancer. Always poised and graceful, this kitten pirouettes around the living room before settling down for the night.

Numa. *M/F.* A lion from such early movies as *The Extra Girl*, Numa was noted for his extraordinary ability to concentrate on the trainer's commands. Naming your kitten Numa probably won't make him a star, but maybe he'll listen better.

Olivier. *M.* Named for Sir Laurence Olivier. The plus side is that a cat with this name has style and class. The downside is that with Olivier, every little thing turns into a drama.

Patsy. *M/F.* The American Humane Association and Motion Picture Executives annually gave a PATSY award to the top animal star of the year (the name is an acronym for Performing Animal Television Star of the Year). If your cat is a real star, give him or her an Oscar of a name.

Pelenore. *F.* The clown name of Peggy Lenore Williams, who in 1971 became the first U.S. woman circus clown. For the female cat whose antics are more Clown College than Radcliffe.

Pooh-Bah. *M.* Pooh-Bah is The Lord High Everything Else from Gilbert and Sullivan's comic opera *The Mikado.* He's pompous and arrogant and sneers at everything. The name Pooh-Bah is now commonly used for everyone's favorite know-it-all.

Princess Tiger Lily. *F.* In *Peter Pan,* Tiger Lily was an Indian princess who, along with her tribe, lived in Never-Never Land. A cat named Tiger Lily is orange or striped and is a real "princess."

Pyewacket. *M/F.* The 1959 PATSY award winner for his role in *Bell, Book and Candle,* starring Kim Novak and Jimmy Stewart.

Radar. *M.* Radar O'Reilly from *M*A*S*H* seems to know about things before they happen. He's always right there ready to help Colonel Potter. A cat named Radar will always spot things before you do.

Ramar. *M.* From the television show *Ramar of the Jungle,* Ramar owned the jungles in the 1950s. Ramar was played by Jon Hall and he kept things in that savage environment on an even keel. A cat named Ramar will do the same for your neighborhood.

Rhubarb. *M/F.* Rhubarb, the fourteen-pound alley cat from the movie *Rhubarb,* was the first and only feline to own the Brooklyn Dodgers. The script called for a rather mean-looking and tough cat to play the part and Rhubarb was just that. His real name was Orangey.

Rochester. *M.* This cat is named after Jack Benny's chauffeur and butler, Rochester. For your favorite sidekick.

Rocky. *M.* From the movie of the same name. Perfect for the kitten who loves to fight.

Satchmo. *M.* For the legendary Louis Armstrong. A cool cat named Satchmo will jazz up your life.

Scaramouche. *M.* This cat's name is taken from the standard buffoon of Italian comedic opera, the cowardly scamp who always makes you laugh.

Schmoo. *M/F.* Like the ham-shaped animal in Al Capp's comic strip *Li'l Abner*, this cat has a rapturous smile and brings good fortune.

Schnoz. *M/F.* For comedian Jimmy Durante. It can only be hoped that this kitten will grow into his nose.

Sheena. *F.* From the comic strip *Queen of the Jungle*. Sheena was that queen. A good name for a cat who likes to tame the neighborhood.

Slats. *M/F.* When Metro-Goldwyn-Mayer was looking for a corporate symbol that was big, loud, and impressive, they settled on a lion. Slats was the first lion chosen to be their live symbol in black and white.

Sluggo. *M.* Cartoon character and friend of Nancy. This name fits those kitties who are good with their dukes. Back-alley cats, they won't let you down in a tough situation.

Snoopy. *M/F*. This name from the Charlie Brown cartoon is usually reserved for dogs. But it's a good name for a cat who just can't resist snooping around.

Sylvester. *M*. The cartoon cat who had nothing but trouble with Tweetie. If you have a smart yellow bird at home, Sylvester is the name for your kitten.

Tanner. *M/F*. Tanner was the lion used as the living color version of the MGM symbol.

Top Cat. *M*. TC for short. Top Cat was a street cat who knew how to get by in the animated TV show of the same name.

Trixie. *F*. Every cat has a trick or two up her sleeve. But being married to Norton on *The Honeymooners* taught this cat more about tricks than any two- or four-legged creature will ever need to know.

Twiggy. *F*. Like the mod model of the sixties, Twiggy the cat is extremely thin and has long legs and huge eyes.

Wallenda. *M/F*. This cat should have been in the circus. Named after the flying trapeze artists The Great Wallendas, a kitten with this name will fly through your house with the greatest of ease.

Wearie Willy. *M*. The famous circus tramp played by one of the most beloved clowns of all time, Emmet Kelly. Wearie Willy was famous for trying to sweep the spotlight out of the ring. Cats with this name don't have to be tired, but they should be funny.

Winky Dink. *M/F.* Taken from the 1950s children's television show of the same name. Winky Dink was always trying to escape from danger. By drawing on a magic screen placed over the TV image, we were able to help him. For the cat who frequently finds himself in a fix but always manages, with a little help from his family, to escape in one piece.

CREATURES OF HABIT

All cats are creatures of habit, some endearing and some to be endured. Some are night prowlers, some singers, some dedicated nappers. Choose a name that describes your cat's claim to fame. Presto or Pokey, the Milkman or the Phantom, these names are lots of fun.

Adagio. *M/F.* Adagio is the musical cat who moves slowly and gracefully.

AWOL. *M/F.* The military abbreviation for "absent without leave." This cat always stays out longer than you'd like.

Bagpipes. *M/F.* From the wind instrument that wails at Irish and Scottish festivities. Cats named Bagpipes make the same sound just about dinnertime.

Bailey. *M.* The cat you're always begging to come home, as the singer did Bill Bailey.

Basker. *M/F.* Basker knows it's always best to lie in the sun and toast himself so he'll be rested and ready for the evening's activities.

Baskets. *M/F.* Baskets is a kitten with an uncontrollable urge to curl up in any basket of any size, anywhere and at any time.

Bocce. *M/F.* A kitten named Bocce is excellent at bowling. Named for the Italian lawn game, she'll roll anything she can find.

Bowie. *M.* Based on the big knife known as the Texas toothpick. For the cat who likes to use his sharp claws.

Catastrophe. *M/F.* This cat is a disaster waiting to happen, but you love him anyway.

Catillac. *M/F.* A cat with this name wouldn't be seen in anything less than the ultimate luxury car.

Catnip. *M/F.* All cats find this herb intoxicating, but this kitten is especially fond of it.

Chitchat. *M/F.* Meow this, meow that, Chitchat thrives

on small talk. She always has something to say, even if you're not really listening.

Clementine. *F.* "Oh my darling, oh my darling, oh my darling Clementine." A fitting name for a cat who always seems to be "lost and gone forever."

Count Pounce. *M.* Count Pounce is a mouser by trade, but he's been known to pounce on just about anything that passes his way—shoelaces, squeaky toys, and your favorite neighbor's dog.

Curfew. *M/F.* The name for cats who, despite all pleas and protestations, can't make it home before the midnight hour.

D-Con. *M/F.* This cat is death to mice and rats. Named after the commercial product designed to do the same job, D-Con the cat will do it faster and better and is a heck of a lot more fun.

Digger. *M/F.* The cat with a proclivity for digging that's much more acceptable in canine creatures. To college basketball followers, Digger also means the former coach of Notre Dame.

Driver's Seat Kitty. *M/F.* This Kitty was the mascot of The Driver's Seat pub in Southampton, Long Island. Regular patrons at this watering hole for society's rich and famous were always honored when Kitty would join them for a drink at the bar. Although Kitty never touched alcohol, he preferred all his libations served chilled in a martini glass.

Fireball. *M/F.* For the kitten who runs around so fast, you expect the carpet to catch on fire any second.

Firefly. *M/F.* If this hyperkinetic kitten doesn't get a parachute, her nine lives will be used up in less than a week.

Flapjacks. *M/F.* This cat's favorite meal is breakfast.

Gator. *M/F.* Gator is a kitten with an inordinate desire to claw, scratch, and even bite things into oblivion. Especially good for kittens with Florida roots.

Gumshoe. *M/F.* The detective cat. Gumshoe gives new meaning to the word curiosity.

Gypsy. *M/F.* For the cat who loves to wander. It's in the blood — but even gypsies settle down when they find a good home.

Handyman. *M.* A cat named Handyman is able to fix just about anything that ails you.

Hatcat. *M/F.* For kittens who enjoy snoozing in chapeaus.

Hawkeye. *M/F.* This kitten likes to sit in trees and keep watch. From this vantage point, she can spot an open cat food tin half a block away.

Jitterbug. *M/F.* Cats named Jitterbug love to move. Named after the swing era dance music, they can hardly keep still. These cats are tapping their toes and ready to go.

Johnny-Jump-Up. *M.* Not the flower, this Johnny-Jump-Up is the cat who can't stay out of your lap — or anyone else's, for that matter. Be glad you're honored and enjoy the company.

Kilkenny. *M/F.* "To fight like Kilkenny cats" is a well-known Irish expression. A cat named Kilkenny should be tough enough to live up to his name.

Kissimmee Kate. *F.* The smoocher from Florida.

Lutèce. *M/F.* For the kitten who prefers something more gourmet than Tender Chunkies. Named for the well-known New York City restaurant.

Meowchi. *M/F.* Ouch! When this kitten affectionately kneads your arm, her needle-sharp claws go right through your shirt.

Milkman. *M.* The milkman delivered very early each morning, making sure to rattle the empties loud enough to wake the neighborhood. Cats named Milkman are early risers and make sure you are, too.

Moccasin. *M/F.* Like an Indian brave, Moccasin the cat walks silently through your house.

Moonshine. *M/F.* The enterprising mountain cat who spends his evenings down in the hollow, up to slightly illegal activities.

Morningstar. *M/F.* Before sunrise, the morning-star planet shines in the east. A cat named Morningstar is best in the morning, and wants to get going when everyone else in the house can hardly get out of bed.

Mowser. *M/F.* For the cat who brings you mice as little presents.

Napper. *M/F.* A master of the art of snoozing, otherwise known as catnapping.

Nighttrain. *M/F.* Some cats can't seem to get rolling until after dark.

No Fault. *M/F.* For the accident-prone cat. Like the auto insurance business, this cat thinks it shouldn't matter who's to blame for that accident.

Peppermint Patty. *F.* Peppermint Patty is the cat who likes to pat things. She'll gently pat your hand or even tap your nose, she'll push a piece of paper to see if it will move. But it's wise to remember that those soft little paws have very sharp claws.

Peter Podger. *M.* Peter Podger is the slim and frisky kitten who through time and aging has become no longer so.

Phantom. *M/F.* Now you see her, now you don't. Don't try to search her out—she only appears when good and ready.

Pokey. *M/F.* For the slow-motion cat who takes extra time to do everything. Like the tortoise who beat the hare, she knows that slow and steady wins the race.

Poser. *M/F.* A quick check of the whiskers, make sure the tail is up straight, everything is clean . . . okay, let's go.

Presto. *M/F.* Presto is the kind of cat who appears from out of nowhere. All of a sudden—Presto!

Puddles. *M/F.* Some cats are said to enjoy swimming. Not Puddles. She likes to wade—in the kitchen sink, in the bathtub . . .

Reveille. *M/F.* For the cat who's an early riser. This cat is named after the military bugle call that signals sunrise and wake-up time.

Rocket. *M/F.* Rocket flies so fast, he leaves only a vapor trail. It can only be hoped this kitten will slow his pace with age.

Scoop. *M/F.* Scoop is the kitten who's first with the news. The moment you step in the door, Scoop's there to tell you all about it.

Scraps. *M/F.* Scraps likes to mix it up with the poodle next door.

Sky. *M/F.* Some cats leap from pillar to post and back again without blinking an eye. Born air cadets, they unnerve everyone but themselves.

Sleepy. *M/F.* One of the seven dwarfs. Good name for the cat who enjoys more than anything else (except perhaps eating) a good snooze in the sun.

Solo. *M/F.* A cat named Solo likes to do it alone. He's cordial, yes, but when it comes to going out at night or exploring the woods, this cat is much happier on his own.

Speed. *M/F.* This kitten can move so quickly that when she strikes you can hardly see her paw move.

Squeaky. *M/F.* Don't you think that those very young kitten noises sound more like squeaks than meows?

Tickets. *M/F.* This kitten has racked up more speeding tickets in a few months than most cats do in a lifetime. If she's not careful, the cat police will have her license.

Ticktock. *M/F.* The clock-watcher who always expects dinner on time.

Tiptoes. *M/F.* Tiptoes is a quiet cat who glides around the house without making a sound.

Tomahawk. *M/F.* This is the Indian cat who's just murder on mice. Any varmints in his yard had better beware.

Trouble. *M/F.* Here comes Trouble. For the kitten with a playful nature.

UFO. *M/F.* UFO (pronounce it "youfo") is your unidentified flying object, hovering somewhere between the refrigerator and the micro before darting off into another space.

Wings. *M/F.* The Wings cat can fly, leaping from the mantle to the bookshelf to the dining-room table and back again.

Wipeout. *M/F.* For cats who lack the usual feline agility and balance. In surfer parlance, these cats, like the Surfari hit song says, "Wipeout."

Zip. *M/F.* This kitten on the go zips here, zips there, zips everywhere.

ZZZs. *M/F.* This cat loves to sleep. Nighttime, daytime, or any time in between, ZZZs is ready for a siesta.

SPORTY CATS

Some cats are all-stars in such feline
sports as high-jumping from the fridge
and batting
rolled-up paper. If
yours is among
them, consider a
name from the worlds of baseball,
football, basketball, hockey, soccer, golf,
or the Olympics. A name like Yogi,
Gretzky, Hoops, Homer, or Rookie will
celebrate your cat's athletic prowess and
your own love of sports.

Abner. *M.* After Abner Doubleday, the inventor of baseball. What better partner to have in the winter hot-stove league?

Air Cat. *M.* For Michael "Air" Jordan of the Chicago Bulls. This cat has unbelievable hang time as he glides through the air.

A.J. *M.* The racing cat named for A. J. Hoyt. 'Round and 'round the room, lap after lap, this kitten goes for the checkered flag.

Ali. *M.* Like Muhammed Ali, this cat floats like a butterfly and stings like a bee.

All-Star. *M/F.* This kitten is the best at everything.

Arnie. *M.* This kitty has more fans than golfer Arnold Palmer during the heyday of Arnie's Army. But it won't spoil him. Arnie will always be the most popular cat in the neighborhood.

Babe. *M.* Babe Ruth. For the "big bambino" who's always hitting a home run with you.

Babe. *F.* For Mildred Ella "Babe" Didrikson Zaharias, one of the greatest athletes of all time and winner of two gold medals in the 1932 Olympics. A cat named Babe naturally excels at all feline sports including crow hop, pouncer, tree climb, litter toss, and scratching post.

Billie Jean. *F.* Billie Jean King, United States Open champion four times and Wimbledon champion six times, is also known for the televised battle of the sexes against Bobby Riggs. For the spunky cat who's destined to teach the neighborhood toms a thing or two.

Broadway Joe. *M.* For Joe Willie Namath, who led the 1969 New York Jets to a Super Bowl victory. This cat is a handsome devil who likes the ladies.

Brunswick. *M/F.* This cat loves bowling. She'll happily roll anything across the floor or the dining-room table.

Cleats. *M/F.* Named after the spikes on the bottom of a baseball player's shoes, Cleats is not reluctant to use his own very sharp claws.

Coach. *M/F.* The Coach is an older cat, a little past his playing prime, but he's dedicated to teaching the local kittens how to play the game.

Cricket. *M/F.* She may be small, but she always plays by the rules.

Daytona. *M/F.* This cat doesn't need a track to break speed records.

Dempsey. *M.* For heavyweight champ Jack Dempsey. Cats named Dempsey are big, loud, and tough.

Dimag. *M.* Joseph Paul DiMaggio, the Yankee Clipper, whose fifty-six-straight-game hitting streak still stands. Some cats are just consistently good.

Doctor J. *M.* For Julius Erving, the MVP basketball player with real class. Good name for the cat who is retired but is still best of breed.

Dugout. *M/F.* This cat spends most of her time watching the others play. Dugout is much more the observer than the participant.

Fenway. *M/F.* The Boston baseball cat, named for the stadium of the Boston Red Sox. Each spring hope springs eternal at Fenway.

Fosbury. *M/F.* The "Fosbury Flop" became famous during the 1978 Olympics. Dick Fosbury went over the high jump backwards and won a gold medal. Cats named Fosbury have perfected an unorthodox jump.

Fumbles. *M/F.* This kitten can't seem to hold on to anything. Toss a catnip mouse to her, and it will get away.

Furlong. *M/F.* Furlong is a real thoroughbred. She's fast and can make the distance. The horse-racing furlong is a distance of 220 yards.

Gerty. *F.* For the kitten who loves to swim. She's named for Gertrude Ederle, the first woman to swim the English Channel.

Golden Bear. *M/F.* The nickname of golfer Jack Nicklaus, Golden Bear is the big yellow-haired cat who can hit golf balls a country mile.

Gretzky. *M.* For Wayne Gretzky, the Great One to hockey fans. Particularly appropriate for cats who treat every small household object like their own hockey puck. Slap shot—and a beauty!

Hank. *M.* For Henry Louis Aaron, Hammerin' Hank, who hit 755 home runs, the most in baseball history.

For the quiet cat who, day after day, year after year, gets better and better.

Highjump. *M/F.* Highjump is the kitten who excels in the jumping events. Your couch, the refrigerator — Highjump will clear them in a flash.

Hobiecat. *M/F.* Hobiecat is a sailing cat. Hobie prefers a catamaran to a schooner just for the fun of it.

Homer. *M/F.* The home-run kitten always makes a big hit.

Hoops. *M/F.* This cat views every crumpled paper towel and every napkin as a basketball. Hoops will try to sink a foul shot off the dining-room table at a moment's notice. First a push or two to get good position, then the shot — good!

Hulk. *M.* For the pro wrestler Hulk Hogan. For very big cats.

Hurdles. *M/F.* A kitten named Hurdles believes that her life is a track meet and your apartment is the track. She specializes in jumping over things while running.

Indy. *M/F.* This cat does five hundred laps around your apartment, with only the occasional pit stop for food.

Juice. *M.* For running back O. J. Simpson. This cat can run like the wind.

Mac. *M.* For the cat who tends to argue. He loves to play, but his temper sometimes gets the best of him.

Magic. *M.* For Magic Johnson, formerly of the L.A. Lakers. Magic cat is magic on and off the court.

Meadowlark. *M.* For Harlem Globetrotter basketball legend Meadowlark Lemon, who always steals the show.

Mean Joe. *M.* Only the toughest felines can be named for football player Mean Joe Green.

Mookie. *M.* For former New York Mets center fielder Mookie Wilson. The fan's favorite, Mookie is the name for a very nice cat who deserves to play full time.

Nadia. *F.* This, the feline gymnast, is named for Nadia Comaneci, the tiny fifteen-year-old Russian who stole our hearts while earning seven perfect scores and three gold medals in the 1976 Olympics.

Noc-a-homa. *M/F.* Chief Noc-a-homa, mascot of the Atlanta Braves, does a war dance each time an Atlanta batter hit a home run. For the cat who roots for the home team and is not afraid to let everyone know.

Nolan. *M.* Lynn Nolan Ryan just keeps on pitching no-hitters even at the age of forty-three. For the cat who is getting older, but is better than ever.

Olga. *F.* For Olga Korbut, the Russian gymnast and gold medal winner who was the first person to do a backward somersault on the uneven parallel bars. Kittens named Olga make this one look easy.

Palooka. *M.* This old puncher is known to take a dive, but he still packs a wallop.

Peewee. *M.* The tiny kitten with big dreams of becoming a major league shortstop. Like his idol Peewee Reese, this Peewee can field and hit.

Rally. *M/F.* A kitten named Rally might look like she's finished, but she always comes back strong.

Rebound. *M/F.* This kitten always bounces back. Off the floor onto the counter, off the counter into the sink, out of the sink onto the floor, ready to start all over again.

Rookie. *M/F.* The newest kitten in the household. Everything is a little difficult because it's so new, but this rookie will someday be an all-star.

Rosey. *M.* For New York Giant Rosey Grier, big and fierce, yet a true gentleman.

Rugby. *M.* Like the British game, which is similar to American football but without the pads, this cat is very rough and tumble.

Scroogie. *M/F.* Scroogie is a baseball term for the screwball and, like the pitch, this cat is different than you expected.

Shark. *M.* Golfer Greg Norman has this nickname. This blond or white-haired cat is very aggressive.

Skeets. *M/F.* When Skeets takes aim, he rarely misses a target—clay or not.

Slalom. *M/F.* The fast cat who loves to schuss through an obstacle course. This cat never goes anywhere in a straight line.

Slugger. *M/F.* A cat named Slugger looks the part. Some dents and bruises, a scar here and there, but a quick look will tell you Slugger could go twelve rounds easy.

Smokin' Joe. *M.* For boxing great Smokin' Joe Frazier. This cat from Philadelphia is one of the greatest all-time heavyweights.

Ty. *M.* Baseball great Tyrus Raymond Cobb, a.k.a. "The Georgia Peach," was so tough that he sharpened his spikes before each game. For the competitive cat who would use an emery board to sharpen his claws if only he could figure out how to do it.

Wheels. *M/F.* From the baseball term for a fast runner, Wheels is too fast to catch. She'll run down the hall and be out of sight before you have a chance to say "cat carrier."

Wilt the Stilt. *M.* For basketball star Wilt Chamberlain. This cat is so tall that he doesn't have to jump to knock things off the kitchen counter.

Yogi. *M.* Yogi Berra, the former Yankee catcher and member of the Baseball Hall of Fame, is known for saying things like, "Eighty percent of the game is pitching, the other half's hitting." For the all-time great cat who sometimes gets confused.

REAL LOOKERS

Huge or tiny, spectacled or booted, rough-coated or fluffy, cats have many distinguishing looks. Tell how your cat makes a special appearance with a name like Goliath, Brillo, Slippers, or Puff.

Big Ben. *M*. For the very large cat who is always home on time.

Big Dipper. *M/F*. A big cat named for the constellation Ursa Major. Cats named Dipper are also fond of fish tanks.

Big Mac. *M.* From the McDonald's hamburger. This is for tough cats only—as all the neighborhood kitties know, it's best to avoid a Big Mac attack.

Blaze. *M/F.* For a distinct marking different in color from the rest of the coat.

Bobtail. *M/F.* You can call this cat either Bob or Bobbie as long as he's the owner of a bobbed tail.

Bonbon. *F.* This pampered pussy looks like she's eaten too many sweets.

Boots. *M/F.* The kitten with four white feet, or four black feet.

Brillo. *M/F.* Not every cat is blessed with a shining, luxurious coat. If yours has a coarse one like the scrubbing pad, try the name Brillo.

Bristles. *M/F.* This kitten's whiskers are short, thick, and very stiff.

Bytes. *M/F.* Like the sound bites of politics and the storage bytes of computers, this cat packs a lot of power into a very small package.

Catkin. *M/F.* Named for the small flower clusters known as catkin because they resemble a cat's tail. For the small and very appealing cat.

Chaps. *M/F.* The hair on this kitten's legs makes her look like she's wearing the leather leggings made famous by cowhands of the Old West.

Chrysoberyl. *M/F.* Chrys for short. This kitten's eyes look just like the yellow or pale green stone known as cat's-eye.

Chunky. *M/F.* Cats with this name are big, thick, and sweet, just like the candy.

Cobby. *M/F.* Cobby describes a cat with a compact body, big shoulders, and a short tail.

Crisco. *M/F.* Like the shortening, a kitten named Crisco is a little fat in the can.

Doughboy. *M.* The cat named Doughboy, like the Pillsbury advertising character, is a pudgy fellow who laughs when you poke him.

Fatcat. *M/F.* A somewhat unflattering name for a slightly overweight feline, or for the cat with big bucks.

Fluff. *M/F.* This small kitten's soft, light, feathery coat makes her look like a ball of fluff.

Goliath. *M.* This Biblical character stood ten feet high in a suit of armor. The fierce warrior met his match in the diminutive David, but his name has remained synonymous for the truly huge person—or cat.

Goodyear. *M/F.* Like the blimp, Goodyear is slow-moving and decidedly rotund. Call him Goody for short.

H.O. *M/F.* H.O. the cat is much smaller than average, but because of his very high quality is in great demand. This name is based on the popular toy railroad trains that were $\frac{1}{87}$ life-size.

Jennifur. *F.* Jennifur is a popular kitten with a beautiful coat.

Jumbo. *M/F.* Jumbo from the Ringling Brothers and Barnum and Bailey Circus was the largest elephant in captivity. Use it for an extra-large (or an extra-small) cat.

Knickers. *M/F.* Favored by old-time golfers, knickers are loose shorts that gather at the knees. This is a good name for the cat with a rough-looking coat over the legs.

Little Dipper. *M/F.* For the kitten who's a tad on the small size. Kittens with this name sometimes surprise everyone and grow up to be Ursa Major or the Big Dipper.

Lo Yo. *M/F.* For the svelte cat. Lo Yo was the original frozen yogurt dessert, introduced by Carvel.

Marbles. *M/F.* Cat's-eye marbles were always most valued as the prettiest, and seemed to shoot the straightest.

Megaton. *M/F.* Some cats are big and some cats are large, but a cat named Megaton is really huge.

Mittens. *M/F.* For a black cat with two white front paws. A cat named Mittens O'Malley is buried next to Richard Nixon's dog Checkers at the Bide-A-Wee pet cemetery in Wantagh, Long Island.

Moby. *M/F.* For a whale of a cat—huge and preferably white.

Nubbin. *M/F.* A kitten named Nubbin is a little small for her age, but don't count her out. She's likely to be a late bloomer.

PB&J. *M/F.* For the peanut-butter-colored cat. The name honors the peanut butter and jelly sandwich.

Peanuts. *M/F.* A smaller than average kitten.

Peepers. *M/F.* Jeepers, creepers, this cat has beautiful eyes.

Penguin. *M/F.* For the cat with a black coat and white chest.

Pinocchio. *M/F.* This cat doesn't need to tell a lie to have a big nose. From the story by Carlos Collodi.

Pins. *M/F.* These pins are legs. They're long and thin and belong to the kitten who's growing just a tad too fast for the rest of his body.

Puff. *M/F.* Like the pastry, not the dragon. Ideal for long-haired, light, fluffy cats.

Rapunzel. *F.* The beautiful long-haired cat. From the fairy tale in which Rapunzel, trapped in the tower, lowers her hair out the window for her lover to climb.

Shades. *M/F.* The light-colored kitten with dark patches around her eyes.

Size Four. *F.* Size four is quite petite. Remember, though, a kitten named Size Four is likely to be a cat named Size Ten in a matter of months.

Slinky. *M/F.* Like the toy with 66.6 inches of curved wire, once in motion this flexible kitten moves effortlessly and seemingly without a bone in his body.

Smackers. *M/F.* These days all the models want big, full lips. For a kitten, Smackers sure does have them.

Snowshoe. *M/F.* For cats with huge feet.

Soupçon. *M/F.* Soupçon is a mere trace of a kitten, but filled with Gallic charm.

Spats. *M/F.* For the cat with white feet. Also appropriate for cats who simply can't get along with their neighbors.

Specs. *M/F.* This is the name for a cat who looks like he's wearing glasses.

Spot. *M/F.* Aside from being the name of the Munsters' fire-breathing dragon, this is a tried and true name for a spotted cat.

Stache. *M.* This cat's full whiskers look like they came off the tenor in a barbershop quartet. The mustache may even have a little twirl at the ends.

Tiger. *M/F.* On the outside, Tiger is orange with dark stripes. On the inside, she's the ferocious and indomitable ruler of the jungle.

Tom Thumb. *M.* Like Tom Thumb, the English dwarf of legend, this name is used for the cat who is small in size but, naturally, big in heart.

Tux. *M.* For the black and white kitty who's always dressed for the occasion.

Tweeds. *M/F.* This name is based on the rough woolen fabric used for coats and jackets. Cats named Tweeds have rough coats and prefer human friends who smoke pipes and teach English Lit.

Wellies. *M/F.* Known formally as Wellington, this kitten always has his boots on.

Whiskers. *M/F.* If there were ever a competition for the longest, this kitten would win paws down.

Whit. *M/F.* For the diminutive cat—a whit is the smallest particle of anything.

LEGENDARY CATS

Many cats are legends in their own time.

They're as handsome as Adonis, as clever as Merlin, or as strong as Atlas. They'll be proud to have the name of a Greek, Roman, Norse, or Egyptian god; a Biblical hero; or a character in an Irish myth or American legend.

Adonis. *M.* Greek myth. A very handsome fellow, Adonis was loved by both Aphrodite and Persephone and was finally killed because of it. When his blood touched the ground, anemones immediately grew on the spot. A good name for a cat who is extremely handsome and is often in trouble as a result.

Ambrose. *M.* Named for St. Ambrose, the fourth-century Italian saint who believed that animals have souls.

Andromeda. *F.* Greek myth. As Andromeda was about to be executed, she was saved by a hero. All those who have saved a cat from danger, please raise their paws.

Aphrodite. *F.* Greek myth. Aphrodite, daughter of Zeus, was the goddess of beauty and love.

Apollo. *M.* Greek myth. Son of Zeus, Apollo was the god of the sun, light, music, and prophecy.

Artemis. *F.* Greek myth. Artemis, daughter of Zeus and twin of Apollo, was the goddess of hunting. The Romans knew her as Diana.

Athena. *F.* Greek myth. This goddess was a brave warrior. The Roman equivalent was Minerva.

Atlas. *M.* Greek myth. Atlas held up the world with his head and shoulders. For the kitten who looks like he's going to be a bruiser.

Babe. *M/F.* American legend. Paul Bunyan, the huge lumberjack, had a giant blue ox named Babe. Babe was so big that the Black Hills of Dakota were used as his gravestone. For your huge cat.

Banshee. *F.* Irish folklore. A banshee is a wailing woman who foretells death or sadness. For the cat who cries sorrowfully in the night.

Bastet. *F.* Egyptian myth. The daughter of Isis and Osiris, this was the cat goddess of the sun, the moon, and love. She was sometimes called Pasht or Bast.

Beowulf. *M.* Danish legend. This invincible warrior slew the terrible monster Grendel and thus saved the people of Denmark. Cats named Beowulf are fierce and brave.

Big Foot. *M/F.* American legend. For your really big and really elusive monster.

Bubastis. *M/F.* This city was the center of cat worship in Egypt around 900 B.C. A yearly cat festival was held there. This cat could be Buba for short.

Ccoa. *M/F.* Native American myth. Ccoa is the Quechua tribe's evil cat spirit. This gray cat with gray stripes is greatly feared and must be constantly placated.

Charmian. *M/F.* Egyptian legend. According to legend, this was the name of Cleopatra's favorite cat. A "charming" name for your own cat.

Clotho. *F.* Greek mythology. Clotho was one of the fates, powerful goddesses who determined the life patterns of all humans. Clotho was the goddess who spun the web of life. For the cat who in her own little way tries to shape your family's pattern.

Dionysius. *M*. Greek myth. The son of Zeus, he was the god of grapevines and wine. He was also the fertility god. Cats named Dionysius just want to have fun.

Endymion. *M*. Greek myth. Endymion was a very beautiful shepherd boy who fell into a trance when he was kissed by the moon. He remained in the trance forever, never aging, as beautiful as the day he was kissed. For your kitten who never grew up.

Finn. *M*. Irish legend. Finn Mac Cool the Irish giant was as well known for his bravery as for his size. This is a good name for a very large cat who does well in battle.

Flora. *F*. Roman myth. The goddess of springtime, Flora brought the flowers and fruit. This is the name for the lovely, gentle cat who is content to just watch things grow.

Galahad. *M*. English legend. Galahad, son of Sir Launcelot, was the holiest knight of the Round Table. He was able to recover the Holy Grail, bringing the greatest glory to Logres. For the extraordinary cat who lives a life dedicated to the search.

Gawain. *M*. English legend. Sir Gawain was one of the bravest and noblest of King Arthur's knights of the Round Table. His most famous battle—with the

Green Knight—was really a test of virtue. To be named Gawain, a cat must be good as well as brave and strong.

Hades. *M.* Greek myth. Hades, Zeus's brother, ruled the underworld. In Roman mythology, he became Pluto or Dis. Being in charge of death did not improve his personality. For the rat-hating cat who wields a mighty scythe.

Hephaestus. *M.* Greek myth. The god of crafts, fire, and warmth. He was lame but was a wonderful artisan who created many beautiful things. This name is for the special cat who, despite his handicap, creates beauty around him.

Hercules. *M.* Greek myth. This god, also known as Heracles, performed amazing feats with his super-human strength. This name is for big, strong, macho cats.

Hermes. *M.* Greek myth. This god, known in Roman myth as Mercury, was a clever messenger. The son of Zeus, he was also the god of wealth and fortune. For the kitten born with a silver spoon in his mouth.

Hestia. *F.* Greek myth. Hestia was the virgin goddess of family and peace. This name is perfect for a lovely and mild cat who is most content at home with friends and family.

Icarus. *M.* Greek myth. The kitten who flies too close to the stove. When the mythological character flew too near the sun, his wax wings melted and he fell into the sea. Icarus the cat, whose coat is made of fur, instead will land in the kitchen sink.

Ishtar. *F.* Babylonian myth. A Babylonian goddess who represented sexuality. She was understandably quite popular and had a strong influence on both beasts and men. Judging by the number of kittens in the world, cats don't need any help in this area.

Isis. *F.* Egyptian myth. The wife of Osiris, this goddess and sorcerer performed many good works. She had a large following. For the kitten whose goodness wins the hearts of all who know her.

Jezebel. *F.* Biblical figure. Married to King Ahab, Jezebel was infamous for her worship of the deity Baal and idols. A kitten with this name is both cocky and shameless.

Joshua. *M.* Biblical figure. He defeated many nations and kings while leading the Israelites across Jordan after the death of Moses. In his most famous victory, he blew a ram's horn and God made the walls of Jericho come tumbling down. Even though you never expected it, Joshua has made the walls of your heart come tumbling down, too.

King Arthur. *M.* English legend. Arthur pulled Excalibur from the stone and went on to bring together the knights of the Round Table at Camelot. A cat with this name is noble, brave, and born to lead.

Li Shou. *M/F.* Chinese myth. This cat god is highly revered because a cat, with superior night vision, can ward off the evil spirits that tend to come after dark.

Maneki-Neko. *F.* Japanese myth. The enchanting female cat who brought well-being and happiness. Maneki-Neko is represented with her right foot raised to eye level.

Mau. *M/F.* Egyptian myth. An ancient Egyptian cat god.

Medusa. *F.* Greek myth. Medusa, with snakes for hair, is the best known of the Gorgons, three horrible sisters who could turn men into stone with just a look. Sometimes your cat looks at *you* in that way.

Merlin. *M.* English legend. The magician who taught and guided the young King Arthur. When Arthur became king at fifteen, Merlin continued to serve as his soothsayer and wizard. This name is for the cat who is guiding your future.

Midas. *M.* Greek myth. Midas wished that everything he touched would turn to gold. His wish was granted, but unfortunately this even included his food. Good name for the cat who wants it all.

Mjölnir. *M/F.* Norse legend. Mjölnir was Thor's magic hammer, which, when thrown to smite his enemies, would always return to Thor's hand. A cat named Mjölnir will always return home at night.

Narcissus. *M.* Greek myth. Narcissus was so beautiful that everyone who saw him fell in love with him, but he was so proud he would have nothing to do with any of them. Artemis caused him to fall in love with his own reflection. A cat named Narcissus loves to look at himself in mirrors or ponds.

Neptune. *M.* Roman myth. The brother of Zeus, Neptune was the god of the sea and usually carried a trident. His foul moods could bring on bad weather and storms, so this is a good name for a tempestuous cat.

Nessie. *M/F.* Short for the Loch Ness monster. Only reclusive kittens need apply.

Nimrod. *M.* Biblical figure. In the book of Genesis, Nimrod is the mighty hunter. A cat named Nimrod is likely to keep your house clear of rodents and any other uninvited guests.

Niner. *M/F.* Because all cats are said to have nine lives. (San Francisco Forty-niners fans also like this name.)

Odin. *M.* Norse myth. Odin was the Norse god responsible for wisdom, poetry, and magic. He was blind in one eye. Cats named Odin might also be blind in one eye, might be very wise, or might even be both.

Orpheus. *M.* Greek myth. Orpheus was the greatest musician of the Greek world. His music was so powerful that it could tame wild beasts, change the course of rivers, and enchant anyone or anything. A simple meow from a cat named Orpheus will change your life forever.

Osiris. *M.* Egyptian myth. In the underworld Osiris was the judge of the dead, but he was also a god of vegetation and of nature who helped to civilize the world. Most cats are rather judgmental, but they help to civilize us all.

Patrick. *M.* Irish legend. St. Patrick is the patron saint of Ireland. It's said that he drove all the snakes from the Emerald Isle. A cat of this name, however, is more likely to focus his attention on mice.

Pecos Bill. *M.* American legend. Named after the western cowboy who taught all cowpokes everything they know.

Pixie. *M/F.* English legend. This cat is named after the small spirits or fairies of England whose greatest pleasure is to play tricks on people.

Prometheus. *M.* Greek myth. The wisest of the titans, who were giant in size and achievements.

Pygmalion. *M.* Roman myth. Pygmalion was a sculptor who fell in love with his creation, a marble statue. He prayed to Venus to make it come to life, which she did. *Pygmalion* by George Bernard Shaw was the play upon which *My Fair Lady* was based. Pygmalion is for the little kitten who brought you to life when you took him home.

Ra. *M.* Egyptian myth. In the morning, this sun god was a child, in the afternoon a man in his prime, and in the evening an old man. That sounds like a perfectly normal cat.

Shaman. *M/F.* A shaman is a priest who uses magic to cure the sick, uncover the hidden, and control events. A cat named Shaman might use her powers to open porch doors, squeeze into shoeboxes, and see visions.

Sisyphus. *M.* Greek myth. Sisyphus was known for his cleverness and treachery. Always up to no good, Sisyphus was punished in the underworld by being forced to push a boulder up a hill for all of eternity. For your errant kitty, banishment to the underworld of the basement is probably enough.

Terpsichore. *F.* Greek myth. The muse of dancers, Terpsichore is for the clumsy little kitten who will grow up to be a beautiful ballerina.

Thalia. *F.* Greek myth. The name of the muse who inspired comedy is perfect for the kitten who keeps you laughing.

Thor. *M.* Norse myth. The god of thunder. Although of good character, he was very tough on his enemies. Cats named Thor are hell on the neighborhood dogs.

Zeus. *M.* Greek myth. Zeus was the number-one deity of Olympus. The Romans called him Jupiter or Jove. He is often pictured wielding a thunderbolt.

COLORFUL CATS

Names describing color are popular  *because color is one of the first things you know about a kitten. But you don't have to settle for Blacky or Whitey — try Raisin or Blizzard instead.*

Aberdeen Angus. *M/F.* This black cat is named for the world-renowned cattle from Scotland called Aberdeen, or Black Angus.

Ajax. *M/F.* This white cat is named for the household product that cleans things whiter than white.

Albee. *F.* From the Latin word *alb*, the feminine of *albus*, meaning white.

Amber. *M/F.* The cat named Amber is a kind of yellow or maybe orange with perhaps a little brown thrown in.

Argent. *M/F.* Argent is the white or silver color of heraldry. Cats with this name are not only white, but are quite proud of their genealogy.

Avalanche. *M/F.* For the big white cat who comes rushing down the stairs. Watch out—Avalanche!

Blackbeard. *M.* Named for Blackbeard the pirate, this scoundrel has a black coat.

Blackjack. *M/F.* A lucky black cat—like the winning hand in the casino game, he always takes the pot.

Blackout. *M/F.* This all-black cat is named after the day in 1964 when everything in the Northeast went dark. In New York City, cats were stranded in elevators and on subway trains, but they fared better than most because of their superior night vision.

Blacky. *M/F.* Blacky is the traditional black cat name. Among the many cats with this name was Blacky the White House cat of President Calvin Coolidge.

Blizzard. *M/F.* A cat with this name is pure white and comes at you nonstop from every direction. Blizzard's velocity is so great that she is no longer considered just a snowstorm.

Bobwhite. *M.* Bobwhite, the bird, is a quail whose call sounds like his name. If your all-white cat has a meow like a whistle, it's an ideal name—and call him Bob for short.

Buff. *M/F.* Buff is a light yellow or orange kitten (not one who runs around with no fur on).

Butterscotch. *M/F.* This cat is named after the yellow-brown candy. The color may not be a perfect match, but it is a sweet name.

Candidus. *M.* Candidus is taken from the Latin word for "white."

Caracal. *M/F.* From the Turkish word for "black ear." Real caracal cats are wild desert lynxes weighing up to thirty-six pounds.

Carrots. *M/F.* For the kitty with orange hair.

Casper. *M/F.* Casper the cartoon character was, according to the theme song, the friendliest ghost you know. Cats with this name are friendly too, but more to the point, they are white.

Chalky. *M/F.* A kitten named Chalky is usually eggshell white.

Champagne. *M/F.* An effervescent cat the color of the bubbly.

Clorox. *M/F.* This kitty has hair so white it looks bleached. Don't blame her for aping the California surfer look—she was born that way.

Coppertone. *M/F.* For cats who look like they have a nice bronze tan. This is also a fine name for cats who like to bask in the sun.

Creampuff. *M/F.* Creampuff is a big, white, furry kitten who's very easy to get along with.

Cueball. *M/F.* This kitten is not bald, just white.

Darth Vader. *M.* From the villain of the *Star Wars* movies. The Darth Vader cat is dressed all in black and has a less than pleasant disposition.

Drifts. *M/F.* Short for Snowdrift and sometimes called Drifty, this is the name for a cat with an abundance of pure white hair.

Dusty. *M/F.* Good for smoky-gray cats, or for the kind of cat who likes playing in the dirt.

Earl Grey. *M.* A gray cat named for a type of tea. The original Earl Grey was given the recipe after a trip to China.

Ebony. *M/F.* For a dark or black cat. Taken from the Old World hardwood trees of the same name.

Eclipse. *M/F.* This cat is so black that she can block out the moon or even the sun.

Flurries. *M/F.* Flurries is a white kitten who's not nearly wild enough to be called Storm or Blizzard.

Frosty. *M/F.* This cat is named after Frosty the Snowman. Frosty is a good handle for any white cat.

Ginger. *F.* The name Ginger is based on the strong brown color of the aromatic spice. In England, "ginger-haired" means orange or red instead.

Goldilocks. *F.* Taken from the children's story "Goldilocks and the Three Bears." A kitten with this name has long, yellow hair and will always find the bed that's not too hard and not too soft, but just right.

Goldrush. *M/F.* The forty-niner kitten with a bright and shiny yellow coat.

Guinness. *M/F.* A cat named Guinness, like the famous Dublin stout, is a deep, dark color. Like the stout, he is also known for his strong and robust character.

Henna. *M/F.* Henna is the cat with just a touch of red in her coat. This name is taken from the reddish-brown hair dye derived from the henna plant.

Hershey. *M/F.* Hershey is the name for the chocolate-colored cat who gives you chocolate kisses.

Ice. *M/F.* For the white cat, or one with icy blue eyes and nerves of steel. Then again, this name could be for the cat who likes diamonds.

Igloo. *M/F.* Igloo or Iggy is the white cat from the Arctic.

Inkberry. *M/F.* Inkberry, the dark or black cat, is named after a holly tree with black berries.

Inkspot. *M/F.* The inky-black cat, but not necessarily one whose singing qualifies him for membership in the classic singing group.

Ivory. *M/F.* The white cat with an ear for music.

Janelle. *F.* For Janelle Commissiong from Trinidad-Tobago, the first black Miss Universe. For dark beauty queens.

Jet. *M/F.* This cat's name is based on the velvet black coal that is often used in making jewelry. It doesn't hurt for a cat named Jet to be quick on his feet.

Johnnie Walker. *M.* Johnnie Walker is a smooth, full-bodied Scotch whiskey. There's Johnnie Walker Black and Johnnie Walker Red. This name is for a very manly cat.

Julius. *M.* Orange Julius is an orange juice and vanilla ice-cream drink, or an orange tabby.

Juneau. *M/F.* The white cat named for the Alaskan capital, where snow is a way of life.

King Cotton. *M/F.* This cat's name is based on what was the most important crop of the South, king cotton. King Cotton the cat is big, bold, fluffy, and white. A kitten named just Cotton is soft, white, and fluffy.

Kleenex. *M/F.* Kleenex is a soft, all-white kitten.

Mahogany. *M/F.* Mahogany wood is yellow-brown or reddish-brown. Used in fine furniture, it has a deep glow.

Mayo. *M/F.* If you have a white cat with this name, you can truly "hold the Mayo."

Midnight. *M/F.* The traditional name for the black cat who is as dark as midnight on a moonless night.

Milkshake. *M/F.* For a vanilla, chocolate, or coffee-colored cat.

Miss Marigold. *F.* Goldie for short, this cat is named for the easy-to-grow, bright yellow flowers.

Nubi. *M/F.* Nubi is a black cat whose name is based on the word Nubia, a black empire situated between Egypt and Ethiopia in ancient times.

Nutmeg. *M/F.* A brown cat who adds spice to your life.

Oreo. *M/F.* The cat named Oreo, like the cookies, is black, white, and very sweet.

Paladin. *M.* For the sophisticated cowboy played by Richard Boone on the television series *Have Gun, Will Travel.* Paladin always dressed in black.

Paleface. *M/F.* Good for cats with white markings on their faces.

Peaches. *F.* Peachy for short. For the sweet orange cat. If she has white feet, call her Peaches 'n Cream.

Pearl. *F.* This cat is greatly prized by her family. Pearl is a white or bluish-white color and, whether natural or cultured, is always a lady.

Pieball. *M/F.* This name is derived from the word "piebald," which is used to describe spotted or blotched black and white cats (and horses, too).

Polarcat. *M/F.* Like a polar bear, this cat is big, white, and woolly.

Popcorn. *M/F.* A fresh white cat who's always jumping around.

Pumpkin. *M/F.* This is the name for your basic orange cat. It's also good for any kitty born around Halloween.

Raisin. *M/F.* A dark-colored kitty.

Raven. *M/F.* From the color of the glossy black feathers of the bird.

Red. *M/F.* For a cat with a reddish coat (kids with carrot tops sometimes acquire the same name). Your cat need not have a fiery temperament.

Rubus. *M/F.* Latin for "blackberry." Rubus is the perfect name for the learned cat who happens to be black.

Rusty. *M/F.* A rust-colored cat—a little orange, a little red, a little brown. Baseball fans will recall Rusty Staub, who attained the nickname "Le Grand Orange" while playing for the Montreal Expos.

Saffron. *M/F.* Like the spice, Saffron is orange-yellow. Just a pinch adds color to your life.

Salty. *M/F.* Salty is the white cat with an off-color sense of humor.

Sandy. *M/F.* A cat named Sandy is usually a yellow-gray mix. Some beaches, however, are white, and others are black.

Shadow. *M/F.* Shadow is a dark or black cat. Shadow is also a good name for a cat who's always right by your side.

Smoky. *M/F.* Smoky is the dark gray or black cat.

Smudge. *M/F.* For the kitten with blurred markings, usually a dark color on white, so she always looks a little bit dirty.

Snow. *M/F.* A cat named Snow is usually pure white unless he lives in a city. In that case an off-white or dirty white cat is a perfectly acceptable recipient of this name.

Snow Job. *M/F.* A salesperson at heart, Snow Job is the white cat who's always trying to put something over on you.

Snow White. *F.* This white kitten's name comes from the fairy tale. Snow White is the fairest of them all. If your Snow White has kittens, some good names for them would be Doc, Grumpy, Sneezy, Dopey, Sleepy, Bashful, and Happy.

Snowball. *M/F.* A kitten named Snowball is a little white fluff ball who melts when you hold her.

Snowcap. *M/F.* A cat named Snowcap may be any color at all as long as there's a white patch on top of his head.

Snowdrop. *M/F.* This kitten is named after the plant with white flowers that often blooms while snow is still on the ground.

Snowflake. *M/F.* For the white kitten who is small but one of a kind.

Snowman. *M/F.* A white cat who enjoys playing outside in the winter.

Snowsuit. *M/F.* This white kitten's name is based on the one-piece bodysuit kids are forced to wear before being allowed out to play in the snow.

Sooty. *M/F.* Name your dusky or black cat for the stick-to-everything black stuff found in chimneys.

Spades. *M/F.* This black cat can be aces or deuces, depending on the luck of the draw.

Stormy. *M/F.* A gray cat, especially one with a mercurial temperament.

Sugar. *M/F.* A cat named Sugar is sweet and brown or white.

Taffy. *M/F.* For the confection made from molasses or brown sugar. Taffy the cat should not only be sweet, but should have a thick and glossy taffy-colored coat.

Tater. *M/F.* This cat is creamy white like a potato.

Whitey. *M/F.* A bit obvious and cute, but a perfectly good name.

Zorro. *M.* For the brave cat dressed all in black, like the swordsman of television and movie fame who came out of the night and helped those in danger.

LITERARY CATS

Some of our greatest authors have also been great cat lovers, from Mark Twain to Colette to the undisputed master of the art of naming cats, T. S. Eliot. For a touch of literary cachet, use the name they chose for a cat in a poem, story, or their own lives. Or make a brilliant literary allusion with a name honoring a human character who's your cat's alter ego, like Huck or Poirot.

Bagheera. *M/F.* Bagheera was the inky-black panther from Rudyard Kipling's *The Jungle Book.* He's smart and bold and very strong. Bagheera bargains for and saves Mowgli the Jungle Boy's life.

Beelzebub. *M.* A name for Satan, from the Bible. Mark Twain used this name for one of his favorite cats.

Blanche. *F.* In *A Streetcar Named Desire* by Tennessee Williams, Blanche's final words are "I have always depended on the kindness of strangers." For the alley cat in your life.

Cat that Walked by Himself. *M.* From Rudyard Kipling's *Just So Stories.* "And all places are alike to me" is this cat's refrain.

Cinderella. *F.* This kitten's name is taken from the fairy tale and is perfect for the stray who finds a home with a prince.

Dinah. *F.* Alice's cat in Lewis Carroll's *Alice in Wonderland.*

Dodger. *M/F.* Like Charles Dickens's character the Artful Dodger, this very clever kitten is street smart and will steal your heart.

Dr. Watson. *M.* The close friend and working partner of Sherlock Holmes. For the good buddy in your life. Loving him will be elementary.

Eliot. *M.* Or call him T.S. The great cat lover and poet certainly deserves one or two named after him.

From T. S. Eliot's
Old Possum's Book of Practical Cats:

Bustopher Jones ("Bustopher Jones: The Cat About Town")—a black cat with white spots, who's very well known in all the right clubs. But la dolce vita has taken its toll, and he's now a twenty-five pounder.

Great Rumpuscat ("The Awful Battle of the Pekes and the Pollicles")—he scatters a fight between the Pekes and the Pollicles.

Grizabella (unfinished poem "Grizabella the Glamour Cat")

Growltiger ("Growltiger's Last Stand")—this barge cat on the Thames is attacked by the Siamese. His mates are Grumbuskin and Tumblebrutus.

Gus ("Gus: The Theater Cat")—a shabby cat who once appeared in many shows.

Jellicle Cat ("The Song of the Jellicles")—these small, merry, black and white cats always enjoy a jig.

Jennyanydots ("The Old Gumbie Cat")—an old striped and spotted tabby who sits and sits.

Lady Griddlebone ("Growltiger's Last Stand")—the object of Growltiger's affection.

Macavity ("Macavity the Mystery Cat")—a criminal cat, altogether the worst of his sort.

Mr. Mistoffelees ("Mr. Mistoffelees")—a small, black cat who is a very good magician.

Mungojerrie and Rumpleteazer ("Mungojerrie and Rumpleteazer")—notorious clowns and cat burglars, they acted so fast that you could hardly tell one from the other.

Old Deuteronomy ("Old Deuteronomy")—a loved and respected cat who has outlived nine wives.

Rum Tum Tugger ("The Rum Tum Tugger")—a cat who always does just as he pleases.

Skimbleshanks ("Skimbleshanks: The Railway Cat")—he's in charge of the sleeper car.

These "pecular and particular names" from "The Naming of Cats" will make a cat proud: Bombalurina, Coricopat, Jellylorum, Munkustrap, Quaxo.

Eliot used to keep a list of other names suitable for cats. It included Noilly Prat (an elegant cat), Carbuckety (a knockabout cat), Tantomi (a witch's cat), Pouncival (a name with Arthurian flavor), and Sillabub (a mixture of silly and Beelzebub).

Fagin. *M.* The cat who specializes in fishing things out of your pockets. He'll teach the neighborhood kittens to do the same. From *Oliver Twist* by Charles Dickens.

Foss. *M/F.* Much-loved cat of Edward Lear, the nineteenth-century English poet who wrote "The Owl and the Pussycat."

Frimbo. *M/F.* Frimbo was the black cat of *The New Yorker* magazine cartoonist Charles Addams. He looked as if he had traveled a long way, so Addams named him Frimbo after *The New Yorker* writer E. M. Frimbo, who loved to travel, particularly by train.

Gangway. *M/F.* The one word in the one-word poem "Short Poem Descriptive of Someone in a Hurry with Something Important on His Mind" in Paul Gallico's *Honorable Cat.*

Ginger. *M/F.* From *The Last Battle* by C. S. Lewis. Ginger is a sly cat who plots against Aslan and is punished. For the kitten who's not as smart as she thinks.

Gink. *M/F.* The cat appearing in many children's books by author Patricia Coombs.

Grimalkin. *F.* The witches in *Macbeth* call on Grimalkin the spirit cat while casting spells. Grimalkin is also a generic name for an elderly female cat.

Heathcliff. *M.* For the brooding, passionate cat who likes to roam the moors, or the local facsimile. From *Wuthering Heights* by Emily Brontë.

Hinx. *M/F.* Hinx belonged to Sir Walter Scott, poet and novelist of Scotland.

Hodge. *M/F.* Dr. Samuel Johnson's cat as recorded in Boswell's *The Life of Samuel Johnson LL.D.*

Homer. *M.* For the ancient Greek author of such epic poems as the *Iliad* and the *Odyssey.* Homer is the heroic, larger-than-life cat who loves an adventure.

Hotspur. *M.* The impulsive and daring cat who is always ready for adventure. The nickname for Henry Pierce, the Earl of Northumberland's eldest son, from Shakespeare's *Richard II.*

Huck. *M.* Mark Twain's Huck Finn was always getting

in scrapes. Twain was a great lover of cats and owned many, including Sourmash, Buffalo Bill, Zoroaster, and Tammany.

Izaak Walton. *M.* After the English author of the fishing classic *The Compleat Angler.* A cat with this name has more than a casual interest in the goldfish bowl.

Jabberwocky. *M/F.* From the poem of the same name by Lewis Carroll. A cat named Jabberwocky loves nonsense and meaningless rhymes and is known to speak a language all her own.

Jeoffrey. *M.* From the eighteenth-century poem "Rejoice in the Lamb (or Jubilate Agno): A Song from Bedlam" by Christopher Smart, a celebration of his cat Jeoffrey, written while Smart was confined in Bedlam, an English insane asylum.

Kitty Kelley. *F.* For the sensationalist author of biographies of Frank Sinatra, Nancy Reagan, and others. This Kitty tells all.

La Chatte. *F.* French author Colette loved cats. One of her favorites was named La Chatte, meaning "the cat" in French.

Lady Jane. *F.* An unladylike and mean cat in Dickens's novel *Bleak House.*

Madame Phloi. *F.* From the cat in the short story "The Sin of Madame Phloi" by Lilian Jackson Braun. Madame Phloi loses her friend Thapthim in a suspicious manner. Loyal to the end, she lures the responsible party to a great fall.

Min. *F.* This name is from "Min Misses a Mouse" by Henry David Thoreau. Min handily catches the mouse yet watches unconcerned as Riordan the cock devours it.

Minnaloushe. *M.* From "The Cat and the Moon" by W. B. Yeats. Minnaloushe is a black cat who is described as "the nearest kin of the moon." This, cat lovers know, is true of them all.

Miss Moppet. *F.* For a cat who, like this Beatrix Potter character, teases mice.

Moses. *M.* From James Herriot's story "Moses the Kitten." Moses is rescued by James Herriot and brought to a farm, where he chooses a most unusual mother—a sow.

Mouschi. *M/F.* In *The Diary of Anne Frank* Mouschi mistakes wood shavings in the loft for his proper litter. The mess filters into the attic, then works its way down into the dining room. How was Mouschi to know?

Mr. Peter Wells. *M.* The cat belonging to English novelist and historian H. G. Wells. It's reported that Peter would invariably leave the room in response to loud or boring conversation.

Mrs. Ribby. *F.* Mrs. Ribby stops by to say hello and borrow some yeast from Tabitha Twitchit in *The Tale of Samuel Whiskers* by Beatrix Potter. For the cat who likes to visit the neighbors.

Mysouf. *M.* French novelist Alexandre Dumas's cat, who walked him partway to his office each morning,

then met him at the same spot at the end of each
working day.

Nellie. *F.* From *Nellie, A Cat on Her Own* by Natalie
Babbitt. Nellie starts life as a marionette. But when
she meets Big Tom the cat, magic happens.

Nerone. *M/F.* One of two cats belonging to W. H.
Auden. The other cat's name was Rhadame. T. S.
Eliot wrote to Auden saying that he didn't approve
of their names and thought that Ponsonby and Phil-
limore would be more suitable.

Norton. *M.* The cute, self-reliant, well-traveled star of
Peter Gethers's *The Cat Who Went to Paris*. Norton
was named after Art Carney's character in *The
Honeymooners*.

Pluto. *M.* From "The Black Cat" by Edgar Allan Poe.
Pluto comes back after a horrible death to haunt his
master and ultimately alerts the authorities to a
murder. For the cat who is quite capable of taking
revenge.

Poirot. *M.* Name the cat who's always snooping around
after Agatha Christie's great detective Hercule
Poirot. Name the female version Miss Marple.

Prince Hal. *M.* The wild and reckless kitten who will
mature into true nobility. From William Shakespeare's *Henry V.*

Proust. *M.* "For a long time I used to go to bed early,"
wrote French novelist Marcel Proust in *Swann's
Way.* For the catnapping kitten who is frequently
found snoozing on your bed.

Puss. *M/F.* This generic name for cats is also well-known from Charles Perrault's "Puss in Boots," written in the sixteenth century. This very clever cat helped his master, a young boy, do very well.

Runyon. *M.* Named after author Damon Runyon, this cat hangs out with a crowd of real characters like Dave the Dude, Nathan Detroit, Apple Annie, Johnny One-Eye, and The Seldom Seen Kid.

Selima. *F.* From "Ode on the Death of a Favorite Cat" by Thomas Gray, the eighteenth-century English poet. She drowned in a tub of goldfish.

Tabitha Twitchet. *F.* From *The Tale of Samuel Whiskers* by Beatrix Potter. She's nervous and anxious because she's always losing her kittens. For the older cat who's becoming quite forgetful.

Tigger. *M/F.* From the character in A. A. Milne's children's classic *Winnie the Pooh*. For the cat who looks like a tiger. Even better if the cat is also a finicky eater, as the original Tigger ate only extract of malt for breakfast, lunch, and dinner.

Tolstoy. *M.* Named for Russian novelist Leo Tolstoy, this cat lives a life that's an epic of war and peace. A good name for a Russian Blue.

Tom Quartz. *M.* Dick Baker's cat from the story of the same name by Mark Twain. He's blown straight up in the air by a mine shaft explosion.

Ulysses. *M.* For Irish author James Joyce's masterpiece. This cat is brilliant, but very hard to understand.

Walden. *M/F.* For Henry David Thoreau's favorite pond. Walden wants to live the simple life with only you, way out in the country.

Webster. *M.* From "The Story of Webster" by P. G. Wodehouse. A black cat of great poise, Webster is able to produce major guilt feelings with just a sidelong glance.

Wee Willy. *M/F.* In the nursery rhyme, Wee Willy Winky ran through the town making sure the children were in their beds. A good name for a little cat who makes the rounds of the beds at night.

Wilhelmina. *F.* Charles Dickens's cat. She was William until he discovered that she was expecting kittens.

WORLDLY CATS

Is your cat's spiritual home Dixie, Vegas,

or Rio? Here are names

taken from places and

languages around

the world. Sophis-

ticated cats will

relish names like A

Bientot. If you have a

Siamese, consider such Asian names as

Chopsticks, Haiku, and Sushi. You can

also concoct a name for your cosmopo-

litan cat from lists that present the words

"cat," "beautiful," "black," "orange," and

"white" in thirty-one different languages—

even Esperanto!

A Bientot. *M/F.* French for "so long." For the cat who's always just on her way out for the evening.

Abdul. *M.* Arabic for "son of." A cat named Abdul is usually Persian and proud of his father.

Ainé or **Ainee.** *M/F.* French for "senior" or "elder." Good name for the oldest cat or the one with the most seniority in your household.

Alanna. *F.* From the Irish word for "beautiful."

Aloha. *M/F.* Hawaiian word meaning both "greetings" and "farewell." For the perfect host—she enjoys greeting your guests at the door, and then seeing them out at the end of the evening.

Ami. *M.* French for "friend." What better friend do you have? The female version is Amie.

Amicus Humani Generis. *M/F.* Latin for "friend of the human race." Amicus or Ami for short. It's a bit pretentious, but maybe your cat is, too.

Au Contraire. *M/F.* French for "on the contrary"—the most important phrase in any cat's dictionary.

Bamboo. *M/F.* In India, bamboo is a symbol of friendship.

Beau Geste. *M/F.* French for "beautiful gesture," for the cat who always acts in an appropriate and graceful way.

Beluga. *M/F.* The Russian caviar, for cats with very expensive tastes.

Big Kahuna. *M/F.* In Hawaiian, *kahuna* means "witch doctor." The big kahuna is the unquestioned chief among witch doctors. Question this cat's authority and you risk being put under a spell.

Bon Chat. *M/F.* Means "good cat" in France or anywhere else.

Bonhomme. *M.* French for "good fellow."

Brie. *F.* This district of France, famous for its cheese, sports a good name for a sophisticated kitten.

Cassidy. *M/F.* From the Gaelic word for "clever."

Chopsticks. *M/F.* This Asian cat is named for the slender eating sticks. The name is also good for a cat who likes to play the piano.

D'accord. *M/F.* French for "agreed." This cat is easy to get along with.

Dixie. *M/F.* For the cat who lives way down South in the land of cotton.

Eureka. *M/F.* Greek for "I have found it." For the cat who loves a game of hide and seek.

Faustus. *M/F.* Instead of the common name Lucky, use the Latin version.

Ferus. *M/F.* Latin for "wild"—as wild as that cute little ball of energy you just brought into your home.

Fez. *M/F.* A red felt hat with a tassel, worn in Morocco and by Shriners. This name is a natural for the Middle-Eastern kitten with style.

Frisco. *M/F.* For the beautiful city by the Bay. Not even an earthquake can keep this kitty down.

Georgia. *F.* Like the song popularized by Ray Charles, Georgia is always on your mind.

Gib. *M.* Nickname for Gilbert. Gib is a name for a neutered male cat in Scotland.

Haiku. *M/F.* A very refined and sensitive kitten, named after a very beautiful, stylized form of Japanese poetry.

Harrigan. *M.* For the Irish cat you'll never have to say a word against.

Hoshi. *M/F.* Japanese for "star." For an Asian kitten who aspires to be on *Late Night with David Letterman.*

Kabuki. *M/F.* For the kitten who makes short, stylized moves like the Japanese dance.

Koyang I. *M/F.* Korean for "cat."

Little Rock. *M/F.* This kitten is smaller than the tough tom named Rocky, but is cut from the same cloth.

Mach-Bagral. *M/F.* Bengali for "fishing cat." Real mach-bagrals are wild cats who prowl in and around the water searching for prey. Your Mach-Bagral might instead be fascinated by the goldfish bowl.

Magnolia. *F.* A good name for a sweet cat from the deep South, where trees of the same name bloom so abundantly and fragrantly each spring.

N'est-ce Pas. *M/F.* French for "Isn't it so?" Be smart and just say yes.

Nuit Blanche. *M/F.* French for "white night" or a poor night's sleep. For a white cat who's active when you're trying to sleep at night. Blanche for short.

Nyet. *M/F.* Russian for "no." This cat can be stubborn at times.

Rio. *M/F.* The Brazilian city famous for its Copacabana Beach and the samba. For the cat who believes that life is nothing but a Carnivale.

Roi. *M.* French for "king." The lion is king of the jungle, as the cat is king of his house. Try to accept it gracefully.

Sahib. *M.* In colonial India, the natives used this word meaning "master" or "sir" when speaking to someone of status. We all know your cat's the master — go ahead, name him Sahib.

Semper Fidelis. *M/F.* Semper Fi for short. The motto of the U.S. Marine Corps, Latin for "always faithful," is a perfect name for any cat.

S'il Vous Plait. *M/F.* For the polite cat who always asks, "If you please."

Sushi. *M/F.* For the raw fish served at Japanese sushi bars. Cats love fish any way they can get it. This is a cute name for a trendy Asian cat.

Tabby. *F.* A generic name usually reserved for a domestic female cat. It's said to have originated with the patterned silk called "tabbi" once exported from England.

Tex. *M.* Big, tough, and walks with a swagger. Howdy, partner.

Tirgillo. *M/F.* Mexican for "little tiger" or "ocelot." Tirgillo is the name for a striped kitten who is more than a little rough around the edges.

212. *M/F.* This hip cat from New York City won't settle for any other area code.

Vegas. *M/F.* Short for Las Vegas. Cats named Vegas are gamblers at heart.

A WORLD OF WAYS TO SAY "CAT"

Language	Beautiful	Black	Orange	White	Cat
Arabic	Gamil	Aswad	Bourtougal	Abyad	Qit
Czech	Krasny	Cerny	Pomeranc	Bily	Kocka
Danish	Skon	Sort	Appelsin	Hvid	Kat
Dutch	Mooi	Zwart	Sinnaasappel	Wit	Kat
Eskimo	Inekonartok	Krernertok	Paunrak-Koksortok	Kakortok	Pussi
Esperanto	Bela	Nigro	Orango	Blanko	Kato
Finnish	Kaunis	Musta	Appelsiini	Valkoinen	Kissa
French	Beau	Noir	Orange	Blanc	Chat
German	Schon	Schwartz	Apfelsine	Weiss	Katze
Greek	Ore'os	Ma'vros	Portoka'li	A'spros	Ga'ta
Hawaiian	Nani	Eleele	Alani	Keokeo	Popoki
Hebrew	Yafeh	Schachor	Tapus	Lavan	Chatul
Hungarian	Szép	Fekete	Narancs	Fehér	Macska
Indonesian	Bagus	Hitam	Manis	Putin	Kutjing
Irish	Álainn	Dubh	Flannbhuf	Bán Geal	Cat

Language	Beautiful	Black	Orange	White	Cat
Italian	Bello	Nero	Arancia	Bianco	Gatto
Japanese	Utsukushii	Kuroi	Orenji	Shiroi	Neko
Latin	Pulcher	Ater	Arausio	Albus	Feles
Norwegian	Skjønn	Svart	Appelsin	Hvit	Katt
Polish	Piękny	Czarny	Pomarańcza	Biały	Kot
Portugese	Belo	Prêto	Laranja	Branco	Gato
Rumanian	Frumos	Pisică	Portocală	Alb	Negru
Russian	Krasívi	Chórni	Apelsín	Byéli	Kóshka
Serbo-Croatian	Lep	Crn	Pomorandža	Bijeli	Mačka
Spanish	Hermoso	Negro	Naranja	Blanco	Gato
Swahili	Zuri	Eusi	Chungwa	Eupe	Paka
Swedish	Vacker	Svart	Apelsin	Vit	Katt
Thai	Ngahm	Dahm	Sohm	Kow	Maa-oh
Turkish	Guzel	Kara	Portakal	Beyaz	Kedi
Vietnamese	Dep	Den	Quá Cam	Trüng	Con meo
Yiddish	Schehn	Schvarts	Marants	Veiss	Kats

H I S T O R I C A L
C A T S

Does your cat have something in common with Churchill, Einstein, Davy Crockett, or Mata Hari? Then, Pilgrim, in this category your name search may be ended.

Abe. *M.* Like Abraham Lincoln, tall, gangly, and dressed in black.

Alexander. *M.* Your Alexander the Great is always looking for new worlds to conquer.

Annie Oakley. *F.* This expert shot became a legend as the star of the Buffalo Bill Wild West Show. For the kitten who puts on her own Wild West show.

Bede. *M.* A serene kitten who would be at home in a monastery, like The Venerable Bede, English scholar and saint.

Belle. *F.* Cattle rustler Belle Starr became legendary for her daring raids on ranches throughout Oklahoma. For your fearless raider.

Billy the Kitten. *M.* For the meanest, rootin-tootinest feline this side of Dodge City.

Black Hawk. *M.* The chief of the Sac, who said that land could never be sold since it belonged to everyone. Cats, sharing this belief, go wherever they like.

Bluegrass. *M/F.* Daniel Boone's cat, probably named after Kentucky, the Bluegrass State.

Brennan. *M.* For Irish hero William Brennan, celebrated in the song "Brennan on the Moor." For the cat who is, as the lyrics say, "brave and undaunted."

Buffalo Bill. *M.* For the western hero William Frederick Cody. Mark Twain used this name for one of his favorite cats.

Calamity Jane. *F.* Martha Jane Canary was a pony express rider and cavalry scout. For the adventurous kitten.

Churchill. *M.* Like Winston Churchill, this cat is solid and resolute. During World War II, the prime minister had a cat named Jock; Churchill was so fond of him that Jock took his meals and even attended meetings with Churchill.

Cleopatra. *F.* The kitten who uses her beauty and charm to rule your household.

Confucius. *M.* For the philosopher cat who seems to be telling you profound things.

Crockett. *M.* Davy, that is. Born on a mountaintop in Tennessee, this woodsman, congressman, and genuine American hero was said to make up his mind about what was right, and then go ahead and do it. Cats are like that, too.

Diamond Jim. *M.* Like Diamond Jim Brady, this cat is a celebrated bon vivant with a very large waistline.

Edison. *M.* This cat is very inventive, like Tom.

Einstein. *M.* You don't have to be a physicist to know that cats are smart. But this name is reserved for the exceptionally gifted.

Forbes. *M.* For the millionaire, collector, and magazine founder Malcolm Forbes. For the well-off cat who has found a very comfortable position in life.

Gladstone. *M.* Florence Nightingale, the nurse and philanthropist, had over sixty cats, each named for a famous man of her time. Among them was a Persian named Gladstone, for the English statesman and prime minister.

Grandma Moses. *F.* This cat is a late bloomer. For the artist Grandma Moses, who took up painting in her late seventies and became world renowned.

Hiawatha. *M/F.* For the Mohawk chief who was known as a lawgiver. Perhaps your cat lays down the law, too.

J. Edgar. *M.* The investicat. Named for FBI head J. Edgar Hoover, this cat is sure to have a file on you, too.

Junko Tabby. *F.* For the cat who loves to climb. Named for Junko Tabei, who on May 16, 1975, became the first woman to climb to the top of Mount Everest.

Kit. *M.* For Christopher "Kit" Carson, explorer of California and other western territories. A good name for your own explorer.

Kitty Hawk. *M/F.* For the place where the Wright brothers took their historic first flight, Kitty Hawk, North Carolina. A cat named Kitty Hawk keeps trying to take flight, starting with a jump off your mantel.

Lizzie. *F.* Lizzie Borden was found not guilty of murdering her stepmother and father with an ax. Even so, most people thought she did it. Only you can decide if the same is true of your kitty.

Lucky Lindy. *M.* The nickname of Charles Lindbergh, who in 1927 became the first person to fly solo across the Atlantic. For the cat in flight.

Machiavelli. *M.* Like the early Italian politico, the devious Mach the cat is fascinated by raw power.

Mata Hari. *F.* This Javanese word for "eye of the morning" was the undercover name of Margaretha Geertruida Zelle, whose activities during World War I made her the world's most famous spy. A kitten named Mata Hari is dark and beautiful, but loyalty is not her strong suit.

Meely. *F.* Amelia Earhart, the first woman to fly across the Atlantic, was called Meely by her family. For the adventurous cat more comfortable in the air than on the ground.

Micetto. *M/F.* Pope Leo XIII loved cats and Micetto was thought to be his favorite. Pope Leo so loved him that he frequently traveled with Micetto safely tucked in his robes.

Mozart. *M.* For Wolfgang Amadeus. Mo for short. A real classic.

Mugwump. *M/F.* Native American for "chief." Naming a cat Mugwump is just a formality since he already knows he is the chief.'

Napoleon. *M.* Don't let his small size fool you—he's building an empire.

Nelson. *M.* Nelson was Winston Churchill's much-publicized cat who, it is said, took refuge under Churchill's bed during the London bombing raids.

Old Mike. *M.* The beloved cat who watched the main gate of the British Museum for almost twenty years.

Papoose. *M/F.* Native American for "baby." Nice for a kitten who likes to be carried around everywhere, as Native American mothers do with their infants.

Picasso. *M/F.* For the cat who's an artist with a different point of view.

Pilgrim. *M/F.* Pilgrim, your search is ended. This name is for the traveling cat who finally found the right home.

Pinkerton. *M.* The detective cat who's always snooping around. Scotsman Alan Pinkerton founded this American detective agency.

Pocahontas. *F.* Pocahontas, daughter of an Indian chief, saved Captain John Smith from execution. For your little Indian princess.

Powwow. *M/F.* Native American for "meeting." Cats named Powwow believe in decision by committee.

Prajadhipok. *M.* Prajadhipok was the King of Siam from 1925 to 1935. Called PJ in familiar settings, this Siamese kitten is true royalty.

Rameses. *M.* Rameses the Great was a king of Egypt. Authors Gloria and James Jones named their Abyssinian Rameses because he looked so regal.

Roy Bean. *M.* Judge Roy Bean dispensed six-gun justice from a court in his saloon. For cats with a matter-of-fact approach to problems.

Samoset. *M.* For the Massasoit Indian chief whose name meant "he who walks over much." A good name for the lucky cat who traveled a great distance before finally finding the perfect home.

Shan. *M/F.* Shan was the Siamese cat who belonged to Susan Ford, the daughter of President Gerald Ford.

Sigmund. *M*. With a cat named Sigmund you'll probably never need Freud's psychoanalysis. But if you ever do, this cat will be happy to curl right up on the couch with you.

Sir Edmund Hillary. *M*. This cat is named after the famous New Zealand explorer and mountain climber. No mantelpiece is too precarious or refrigerator too high for Sir Edmund to climb.

Sitting Bull. *M*. For the Sioux medicine man and chief. This cat loves to sit around and shoot the bull.

Sizi. *M/F*. Sizi belonged to Dr. Albert Schweitzer while he was a missionary in Africa.

Slippers. *M/F*. President Theodore Roosevelt's cat Slippers had six toes.

Spartacus. *M*. The slave, gladiator, and insurrectionist who led an unsuccessful revolt against his Roman captors. A kitten named Spartacus is brave and bold, and believes that freedom is for everyone, especially himself.

Sputnik. *M/F*. For the kitten who sends you into orbit, try Sputnik. On September 24, 1957, this Russian satellite launched the space race.

Sulayman. *M*. For the sixteenth-century Ottoman sultan Sulayman the Magnificent. Good choice for the well-bred Persian in your family.

Tabby L. *M/F*. Tabby belonged to Tad Lincoln, the son of Abraham Lincoln.

Tecumseh. *M.* The name of the Shawnee chief means "shooting star." For your own star kitten who loves to zip around the house.

Tiddles. *M.* The famous cat who made his home in the ladies room of London's Paddington Station.

Tut. *M.* The most famous Egyptian pharoah. Like King Tut, your cat thinks he's a god and a king.

Uncle Sam. *M.* The all-American kitten whose favorite holiday is the Fourth of July. Uncle Sam wants you.

Wampum. *M/F.* The beads or shells used by Native Americans as money. Wampum the cat is of great value to you.

White Heather. *M/F.* One of Queen Victoria's favorite cats, according to Cleveland Amory in his book *The Cat Who Came for Christmas.*

Wigwam. *M/F.* Wigwams were Native American dwellings consisting of long poles covered with bark or rush. A good name for the kitten who likes to cozy up in her own little spot in her own little home.

Wilberforce. *M.* England's Downing Street cat was brought in to resolve a mouse-in-the-house problem and stayed through the terms of four different prime ministers.

Wild Bill. *M.* Western legend Wild Bill, or James Butler Hickok, was a marshal in Abilene, Kansas. You'll know if this name is right for your cat.

Xérxes. *M.* Xérxes the Great was king of ancient Persia. A good name for the Persian in your household.

WELL-BRED CATS

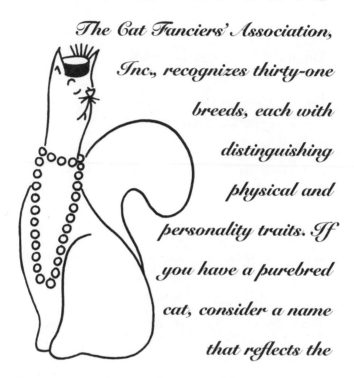

The Cat Fanciers' Association, Inc., recognizes thirty-one breeds, each with distinguishing physical and personality traits. If you have a purebred cat, consider a name that reflects the characteristics or history of your breed. To get your thoughts rolling, here is one name perfectly suited to each breed.

Almonds. *M/F.* For the brilliant, almond-shaped eyes of the Abyssinian. The Aby, usually small and slender, looks like an ancient Egyptian sculpture of a cat. She is one of the most loyal cats and makes an excellent companion.

Anna. *F.* The beautiful, blue-eyed Siamese cat originated in Siam, which is now known as Thailand. It is said that only royalty were permitted to keep these cats. This name comes from the character in *Anna and the King of Siam.*

Bali Hai. *M/F.* The Balinese looks a lot like a Siamese with a long and silky ermine coat. In their good-natured hearts and personalities the two breeds are quite the same.

Chappy. *M/F.* The Cymric is a purebred manx with long hair. Pronounced "kim-rick," these cats, like the manx, have no tail and have a terrific sense of humor. Like Charles Chaplin, these clowns remain young and playful throughout their adult lives.

Cheroot. *M.* Name your Havana Brown cat after a word for "cigar," as Cuba is said to make the best smokes in the world. The breed has a solid brown coat. It tends to be a quiet cat with a very affectionate nature.

Cornelius Rex. *M.* The Cornish Rex is an intelligent cat with large eyes and ears. He has a very soft and wavy coat which distinguishes him from other cats. Call this cat Corny for short. He's the cat who will like you, your friends, your children, and even your dog.

Dancer. *M/F.* The Burmese cat is widely known as the clown of the cat world. He loves attention and always makes it a point to find the spotlight. The "Burmese shuffle," a little dance move, gives our friend his name.

Dots. *M/F.* The Egyptian Mau is the only natural domestic spotted cat breed. It is also one of the oldest breeds, dating back to 1400 B.C., when cats were considered sacred in Egypt.

Dundee. *M/F.* The Scottish Fold cat is from the Tayside region of Scotland, not far from Dundee. The kittens are born with straight ears, but then after several weeks the ears fold forward and down toward the head.

Esther. *F.* The Turkish Van was developed in an area that today includes Turkey, Iraq, Iran, and part of the Soviet Union. Known as the "swimming cats," they love water. Esther Williams was that way, too.

Frère. *M.* From the legend that the original Chartreux breed was formed by the French Carthusian monks. The brothers made a great liqueur, too. These cats are great jumpers and climbers.

Ginnie. *F.* The Bombay cat looks a lot like a very small panther. One look at her shiny black coat, golden or copper eyes, and strong body makes you think that this cat should live in the jungle. Ginnie, however, is named for the much more civilized Bombay gin.

Gorby. *M.* Russian Blues are said to have come from Russia or Northern Europe in the 1800s. This very intelligent cat has a complex personality.

Honk. *M/F.* Honk the Tonk is a less than dignified name for this very intelligent and beautiful cat. Distinguished by their aqua eyes, Tonks are the product of breeding Burmese with Siamese. These cats like to play, and at heart are fun performers.

Hot Spots. *M/F.* The Ocicat is selectively bred to look like a jungle or wild cat. His numerous spots give the impression of an ocelot or leopard. His temperament, however, is very unjungle-like and friendly. Outgoing, devoted, and smart, the ocicat makes an ideal companion.

Jasmine. *F.* The elegant Colorpoint Shorthair has a white or off-white coat, so name her for the white flowers used to make perfume. This breed is sensitive and sometimes a little shy, but is always comfortable with her family.

Joe. *M.* The all-American cat is the American Shorthair. And what better name for an all-American than Joe? These purebred cats are large, mild in temperament, easy to care for, and very friendly.

Kinky. *M/F.* Kinky is named for the type of coat that makes the American Wirehair cat unique. The first litter with the characteristic coarse, springy coat was born in upstate New York in 1966.

Kittery Kat. *M/F.* The Maine Coon cat is a native of the state o' Maine. Her long hair suits her well for the tough New England winters. Some people joke that the Maine Coon acquired her long coat when a local raccoon bred with a cat. Kittery is a town on the Maine coast.

Maggie. *F.* The British Shorthair is quite possibly the oldest natural English breed. Bloodlines for this compact and reserved cat are said to go all the way back to ancient Rome. Maggie the cat is named for former Prime Minister Margaret Thatcher, who left her mark on England and the world.

Pasha. *M/F.* The Exotic Shorthair is a cross between a Persian and an American Shorthair. He combines the temperament of a Persian with the shorter, easy-to-care-for coat of the American Shorthair. The name Pash is a combination, too.

Peter Pan. *M.* It's said that the Javanese cat, like Captain Hook's arch enemy Peter Pan, never grows up. She remains kitten-like forever.

Sevens. *M/F.* The Korat is the good-luck cat of Thailand. Silver blue with bright green eyes, the Korat breed was named by King Rama V. These cats have well-developed senses and dislike loud noises or commotion. Any cat named Sevens is lucky, and a Korat cat named Sevens will be followed by who knows how much good fortune.

Shah. *M.* Persian cats are one of the most popular breeds in the United States. Originally from Persia, today's Iran, these cats are noted for their long coats. The Shah is the traditional sovereign of Iran and a fitting name for this aristocratic breed.

Shelley. *M/F.* Shelley (Berman) the Birman is a cat with a sense of humor. This cat knows how to tell a joke. Originally from Burma and considered sacred temple guardians, Birmans are large light-colored cats with long, silky coats. The standard requires that all four feet be white.

Sling. *M/F.* Singapore is known in Malaysia as Singapura. The Singapura cat is a natural breed from this relatively small Southeast Asian island. Singapore Sling is partial to late nights and cool, strong drinks.

Sommelier. *M/F.* If Sommelier seems like a bit too much of a name for a Japanese Bobtail, then maybe Corky is a better choice. Both names are based on the breed's distinguishing characteristic—a short tail about four inches long that curls into a tight corkscrew, the basic tool of the wine steward, or sommelier.

Stilts. *M.* The Oriental Shorthair is a medium-size cat with large ears, long neck, and legs that are long and sort of like stilts. They usually have green eyes, although a white Oriental Shorthair may have blue.

Zooie. *M/F.* Once believed extinct, the Turkish Angora was rediscovered in a controlled breeding program at the Ankara Zoo in 1962. The Angora is an intelligent and affectionate cat.

PAIRS AND TRIPLES

Two cats are better than one, and three is better yet. Since multiple kittens need multiple names, here are some classic pairs and triplets that go together like, well, Barnum and Bailey.

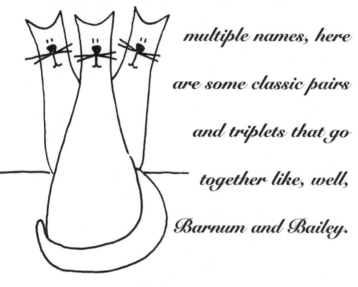

TWO CATS

Aces and Eights. *M/F.* The most infamous two of a kind in poker was Wild Bill Hickok's aces and eights. Aces and Eights was an unlucky pair for Bill, but it could be just the right combination for two much-loved family pets.

Adagio and Allegro. *M/F.* Like the musical terms, one is slow and the other is fast.

Aid and Abet. *M/F.* These two kittens work their naughtiness as a team. By encouraging and helping each other, they will most certainly succeed.

Alpha and Omega. *M/F.* The first and last letters of the Greek alphabet are a good pair for two cats who mean everything to you.

Am and Si. *M/F.* In Disney's *Lady and the Tramp*, these Siamese spoke for an entire breed: "We are Siamese, if you please. We are Siamese, if you don't please."

Ashley and Rhett. *M.* In *Gone with the Wind*, Ashley Wilkes and Rhett Butler are the rivals for Scarlett O'Hara's heart. Television's Vanna White used these names for her cats, who are best friends.

B and O. *M/F.* Cats named for the famous rail line just keep rolling along.

Barney and Fred. *M.* The Flintstones characters. Yabba, dabba, doo! Not for particularly cerebral cats.

Barnum and Bailey. *M/F.* For the cats who turn your house into a three-ring circus.

Baucis and Philemon. *M/F.* From the Roman myth. Baucis and Philemon were an elderly couple who, even though they were very poor, took in the disguised Roman gods Jupiter and Mercury. As a reward the gods offered to grant a favor. Their only wish was that they be allowed to die together, a wish that was granted by the gods.

Bon Jour and Bon Soir. *M/F.* French for "good day" and "good evening." Together, they make your whole day happy.

Chuck and Di. *M/F.* The prince and princess joined in a fairytale wedding.

Cisco and Pancho. *M.* In the television western *The Cisco Kid,* Cisco and his sidekick Pancho fought for truth, justice, and the western way.

Edward and Wallis. *M/F.* King Edward VIII abdicated from the English throne to marry his true love, Wallis Warfield Simpson. For two cats whose love will not be denied.

Ever and Anon. *M/F.* Again and again, over and over, Ever and Anon never let up. Eventually, these kittens will grow up and you'll miss the good old days. Maybe.

Felix and Oscar. *M.* For television's Odd Couple, Felix Unger and Oscar Madison. One is excessively neat, one is excessively sloppy, but despite occasional spats they are the best of friends.

Ferdinand and Isabella. *M/F.* If you want to go exploring, these cats will support you all the way.

Fire and Brimstone. *M/F.* These old-fashioned cats are preachers by nature and will frown on everything you really like to do.

First and Ten. *M.* The football cats. They'll have a rough and tumble pickup game anywhere, at any time. You get to be the referee.

Franny and Zooey. *M/F.* From the book by J. D. Salinger. Like his offbeat characters, Franny the cat is spiritually inclined and Zooey is a very thin and handsome actor. If you have a large and very unusual litter, you can name the rest of the kittens after Franny and Zooey's siblings—Seymour, Buddy, Boo Boo, Walt, and Waker. Their last name was Glass.

Gilbert and Sullivan. *M.* W. S. Gilbert and Arthur Sullivan were famous for comic operas including *H.M.S. Pinafore, The Pirates of Penzance,* and *The Mikado.* Even though these cats don't particularly like each other, they do know how to create a rollicking good time.

Ginger and Fred. *M/F.* Ginger Rogers and Fred Astaire exemplified the style of an era. Dance, laughter, sophistication, and fun were all part of their charm.

Hans and Fritz. *M.* Hans and Fritz were the Katzenjammer Kids from the comics. Loosely translated from the German, katzenjammer means "cats' yowl." Both Hans and Fritz, like some kittens we know, were adept at finding trouble everywhere.

Harry and Tonto. *M/F.* Taken from the movie of the same name. Harry, played by Art Carney, was aging, and Tonto was his best friend cat.

Herb and Tootsie. *M/F.* Dagwood and Blondie Bumstead's next-door neighbors.

Hero and Leander. *M/F.* In the Roman myth, Hero was a lovely young woman, Leander a very handsome young man. Each night Leander would swim the Hellespont to meet Hero. But when winter came, Leander attempted to swim the river and drowned. When Hero saw his body on the rocks below, she threw herself off the cliff and onto the rocks so that she would be with Leander forever.

Herself and Himself. *M/F.* These Irish cats know who they are and what they are and their precise standing in the family. Don't even consider arguing with them; they are the master and mistress of the household.

Hugin and Munin. *M/F.* Norse myth. The ravens of the chief Norse god Odin, who flew all over the world to keep Odin posted on all activities. Their names mean "thought" and "memory."

Jekyll and Hyde. *M.* These cats are total opposites, one nice and the other not.

John and Yoko. *M/F.* For John Lennon and Yoko Ono. For two cool cats who do their own thing, musically and in life.

Launcelot and Guinevere. *M/F.* Launcelot was the bravest and strongest of all the knights of the Round Table. Guinevere was the wife of King Arthur. These cats fell in love at first sight.

Lee and Grant. *M.* These cats are named after the Civil War generals Robert E. Lee and Ulysses S. Grant—one from the South, the other from the

North. Cats named Lee and Grant are always doing battle.

Lewis and Clark. *M.* The explorer cats, always expanding their territory.

Liz and Dick. *M/F.* These cats really love each other, but artistic temperaments and the pressures of stardom keep them apart.

Lord and Lady Muck. *M/F.* Spoiled rotten and used to getting their own way, Lord and Lady Muck are unbearable, but they are, after all, family.

Luigi and Mario. *M.* The Mario Brothers of the Nintendo video game. Your kids will spend a lot of time with these cats.

Madison and Jefferson. *M.* For presidential types.

Maggie and Jiggs. *M/F.* From the husband and wife comic strip *Bringing Up Father.* Maggie is a social climber always trying to impress her fashionable friends, while Jiggs just likes to hang out with his lowbrow cronies.

Masters and Johnson. *M/F.* For Virginia Masters and William Johnson, authors of the landmark study on human sexual response. For male or female cats with a keen interest in feline sexuality.

Meum et Tuum. *M/F.* This Latin phrase meaning "mine and thine" is used in property contracts. Is one cat yours, the other your significant other's?

Mickey and Minnie. *M/F.* For the Disney cartoon characters (wonderfully named, even if they are mice).

Mutt and Jeff. *M/F.* Taken from the comic strip of the same name. Mutt is tall and Jeff is short.

Nettik and Tac. *M/F.* "Kitten" and "Cat" spelled backwards.

Odysseus and Penelope. *M/F.* In the Greek classic the *Odyssey,* Odysseus went off on adventures for twenty years, while Penelope, though besieged by suitors, waited for his return. For the wandering, adventurous cat and his loyal and beautiful mate.

Orville and Wilbur. *M.* Orville and Wilbur Wright were the first to fly a plane. Kittens with this name live up to their airborne heritage as they fly from room to room, going where no cat has ever gone before.

Pho and Mia. *M/F.* The first Siamese cats brought to England. The year was 1884.

Popeye and Olive. *M/F.* Popeye the sailor man and Olive Oyl, his skinny sweetheart, are a fickle pair but truly in love.

Punch and Judy. *M/F.* Like the puppets, these kitties fight all the time, with comic results.

Ranger and Tonto. *M.* These cats catch mice the way Clayton Moore and Jay Silverheels caught horse thieves on *The Lone Ranger.* The names are really perfect if one cat looks like he's wearing a mask.

Regis and Kathie Lee. *M/F.* Regis Philbin and Kathie Lee Gifford are the stars of a morning talk show.

Cats named Regis and Kathie are showbiz all the way but really love their family.

Ricky and Lucy. *M/F.* For Ricky Ricardo and Lucille Ball, the bandleader and the comedienne. They were the stars of one of television's most enduring and beloved series, *I Love Lucy*.

Rocky and Bullwinkle. *M.* From the classic cartoon. Bullwinkle was a moose—a fine name for your big cat. Rocky was a flying squirrel—just the name for his slightly out of control but smarter and smaller brother.

Rolex and Timex. *M/F.* The "watch cats." One is slightly more expensive than the other, but both will take a licking and keep on ticking.

Roy and Dale. *M/F.* For Roy Rogers and Dale Evans, the cowboy and cowgirl pair. Great for western cats who would really love to be down on the ranch.

Samson and Delilah. *M/F.* In the Biblical story, Delilah took away Samson's immense strength by cutting his hair. Cats with these names do fine if Delilah the beautiful refrains from grooming the long-haired Samson.

Scylla and Charybdis. *M/F.* These are two equally hazardous cats, named for twin perils (a sea monster and a whirlpool) faced by Ulysses in Greek mythology.

Shall and Will. *M/F.* "I call my cats Shall and Will because no one can tell them apart," said sixteenth-century English dramatist Christopher Marlowe.

Smith and Wollensky. *M.* The steakhouse cats, named for the famous New York City restaurant that serves a steak as big as your plate. These cats know where the beef is.

Stanley and Livingstone. *M.* Sir Henry Morton Stanley and David Livingstone were early explorers of Africa. When Stanley found the missing Livingstone, he uttered the famous line, "Dr. Livingstone, I presume." Stanley and Livingstone the cats will be difficult to contain in your own backyard.

Stars and Stripes. *M/F.* For all-American kitties.

Sticks and Stones. *M/F.* Sticks and Stones may break their bones—if they continue to climb big trees.

Toody and Muldoon. *M.* From television's comedy cop show *Car 54 Where Are You?* Like the original Toody and Muldoon, these cats are definitely not the shoot-'em-up types and they don't catch many criminals.

Tristan and Isolde. *M/F.* Tristan was a knight and Isolde the queen of Ireland. They drank a potion and fell helplessly in love. Cats with these names seem to have done the same.

Tweedledum and Tweedledee. *M/F.* The mirror-image cats who not only look alike but behave the same way, too. From Lewis Carroll's *Through the Looking Glass.*

Yogi and Boo Boo. *M/F.* Based on the cartoon bears,

Yogi and Boo Boo are loads of fun, and are "smarter than the average" cat.

Zelda and Scott. *M/F.* For author F. Scott Fitzgerald and his love, Zelda, who really lived the Great Gatsby life.

THREE CATS

Duke, Willie, and Mickey. *M.* For New York's favorite center fielders. Duke Snider, Willie Mays, and Mickey Mantle played for the Brooklyn Dodgers, New York Giants, and New York Yankees respectively.

Jekyll, Jessup, and Jill. *M/F.* From the poem "Five Eyes" by Walter de la Mare. Jekyll has two eyes, Jessup has two, and Jill has one. They all wait each night in Hans's old mill for rats to appear in the grain bins.

Groucho, Harpo, and Zeppo. *M/F.* The Marx brothers had much in common with cats. They were clever and outrageous, but most of all they were just plain funny.

Michelangelo, Donatello, and Raphael. *M.* Three of the Teenage Mutant Ninja Turtles. The fourth is Leonardo.

Mo, Larry, and Curly. *M/F.* The Three Stooges. These slapstick kittens will do anything for a laugh.

Sunny, Funny, and Money. *M/F.* From the story "A Kindle of Kittens" by Rumer Godden. Sunny is an orange marmalade kitten, Funny is a dark kitten with a wrinkled face, and Money is a handsome kitten who is thought to be valuable.

Tinkers, Evers, and Chance. *M.* The Chicago Cubs renowned double-play combination of the early 1900s. Joe Tinker, Johnny Evers, and Frank Chance were baseball's best. These names are strictly for major league cats.

Veni, Vidi, Vici. *M/F.* From Caesar's famous Latin utterance, which means "I came, I saw, I conquered." With your cats, you know it's the truth.

Wynken, Blynken, and Nod. *M/F.* Cats love a good sleep. From the children's poem by Eugene Field.

TOP CATS

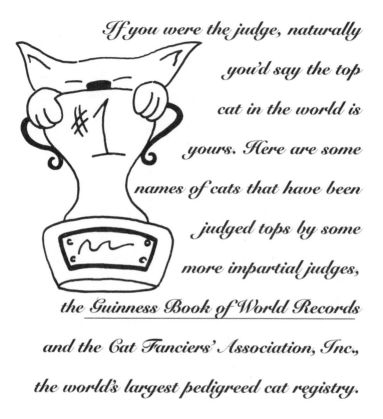

If you were the judge, naturally you'd say the top cat in the world is yours. Here are some names of cats that have been judged tops by some more impartial judges, the Guinness Book of World Records and the Cat Fanciers' Association, Inc., the world's largest pedigreed cat registry.

TOPS IN THE GUINNESS BOOK OF WORLD RECORDS

Bluebell. *M/F.* Bluebell gave birth to the largest recorded live litter of kittens. A Persian from Cape Province, South Africa, Bluebell had a litter of fourteen.

Bull. *M.* A Singapura owned by Carl Mayes, Bull is the most valuable cat on record. Mr. Mayes turned down an offer of $10,000 for Bull, who's considered the best example of his breed.

Charlie Chan. *M.* Charlie Chan, a white alley cat, is the richest cat on record. His owner, Mrs. Grace Patterson, died in 1978, leaving him an estate valued at around $250,000. That's a lot of kitty litter.

Dusty. *M/F.* Dusty has the dubious distinction of having the most number of kittens. By the age of seventeen Dusty had given birth to her 420th kitten.

Ebony-Eb-Honey Cat. *M/F.* Ebony, a male Siamese, was the smallest recorded adult cat. In 1984 at the age of one year, eleven months, Ebony weighed only one pound, twelve ounces.

Edward Bear. *M.* Although the record is unconfirmed, the *Guinness Book of World Records* reports that Edward Bear, a cat owned by Jackie Fleming of Australia, weighed forty-eight pounds.

Himmy. *M.* The confirmed record holder, Himmy was the heaviest domestic cat in history. Weighing in at forty-six pounds, fifteen and one-quarter ounces, Himmy was owned by Thomas Vyse of Cairns, Australia.

Puss. *M/F.* Puss was the oldest cat in history. An English tabby, Puss lived to be thirty-six.

Towser. *M/F.* Towser, a female tortoiseshell, was the greatest mousing champion on record—28,899 killed, an average of three a day for life.

1990 NATIONAL AWARD WINNERS

According to the Cat Fanciers' Association, Inc., the following are the top twenty-five National Award Winners for 1990 in the United States. The categories are: Top Cat, open to both male and female cats; Top Kittens, open to kittens four to eight months of age; and Top Cats in Premiership, open to altered males and females.

BEST CATS

1. **Katrina's Postmarque of Katra.** *M.* Black Persian.
2. **Q-T Cats Danny Boy.** *M.* Red Tabby Persian.
3. **Bajonga's Rusty Knockers.** *M.* Red Persian.
4. **Kitty Charm Fan the Fire of Araho.** *M.* Red Persian.
5. **Copacats Bojangles.** *M.* Black Persian.
6. **San-Toi Yankee Doodle Dandy of Elsk.** *M.* Seal Point Siamese.
7. **Kanab's Luannes's Mahogany Rush.** *M.* Red Tabby and White Maine Coon.
8. **Shanacee Bentley of Nufurs.** *M.* Copper-eyed White Manx.
9. **Ronlyn Barbie Doll.** *F.* Tortoiseshell Persian.

10. **Shechinah Daniel.** *M.* Ruddy Abyssinian.
11. **Adelwies Sometime Lover of Pamel.** *M.* Red Persian.
12. **Shabou Shannon.** *F.* Seal Point Siamese.
13. **Catsafrats Ice Cube.** *M.* Blue-eyed White Persian.
14. **Jovan Yipes Stripes.** *F.* Red Tabby Exotic Shorthair.
15. **Friday's Electra Glide in Blue.** *M.* Russian Blue.
16. **Qitta Jeté.** *F.* Blue Abyssinian.
17. **Maboo's Tiffany.** *F.* Blue Point Siamese.
18. **KJS Miss Abits of Twinshire.** *F.* Cream Point Himalayan-Persian.
19. **Windpegs Snowburst.** *M.* Copper-eyed White Persian.
20. **Kapula Lady in Brown of Heirbourne.** *F.* Havana Brown.
21. **Carocats Kubla Khan.** *M.* Brown Tabby American Shorthair.
22. **Mullodies Sundance.** *M.* Red Persian.
23. **Kotickee's Rassy Sassoul.** *F.* Copper-eyed White Devon Rex.
24. **Nekomo Arata Isozaki.** *M.* Black and White Japanese Bobtail.
25. **Kikicats Answered Prayer.** *M.* Silver Tabby and White Persian.

BEST KITTENS

1. **South Paw Starlight.** *F.* Copper-eyed White Persian.
2. **Jorien's Southern Belle of Rambo.** *F.* Calico Persian.

3. **Kitty Charm's Ice Maiden.** *F.* Copper-eyed White Persian.
4. **Anz Betty Boop of Pajean.** *F.* Black and White Persian.
5. **Nekomo Arata Isozaki.** *M.* Black and White Japanese Bobtail.
6. **Revillion My Oh My.** *M.* Blue-eyed White Persian.
7. **San-Toi Yankee Doodle Dandy of Elsk.** *M.* Seal Point Siamese.
8. **Windborne How Sweet It Is.** *F.* Blue-eyed White Persian.
9. **Nekomo Sabita.** *M.* Red Tabby and White Japanese Bobtail.
10. **Toshika's Sweet Dreams.** *F.* Copper-eyed White Persian.
11. **Catknapp Cardinal Sin.** *M.* Red Abyssinian.
12. **Cacao More Than a Miracle.** *M.* Seal Point Himalayan-Persian.
13. **Leggs Amapola of Mayflower.** *M.* Blue-eyed White Oriental Shorthair.
14. **Oakway Sunkist of Northbrook.** *F.* Red Persian.
15. **Sherecon's Fold on a Minute.** *M.* Silver Tabby and White Scottish Fold.

BEST ALTERS

1. **Attraction's Amy Lou Retton.** *F.* Dilute Calico Exotic Shorthair.
2. **Nekomo Kenji of Kemage.** *M.* Red and White Japanese Bobtail.
3. **Scottish Why Me.** *M.* Brown Tabby and White Scottish Fold.

4. **Keijik's Ten on the Richter.** *M.* Sable Burmese.
5. **Nufurs Nikita of Framor.** *M.* Brown Mac Tabby and White Manx Neuter.
6. **South Paw Peter Pan.** *M.* Copper-eyed White Persian.
7. **Tylona's Morgana.** *F.* Silver Tabby American Shorthair.
8. **Tahame's Hildegarde.** *F.* Copper-eyed White Manx.
9. **Walnut's Rusty Sun at Daybreak.** *M.* Red Abyssinian.
10. **Comesee Brewster of Mymark.** *M.* Blue Point Himalayan-Persian.
11. **Nekomo Michiko of Katoklix.** *F.* Black and White Japanese Bobtail.
12. **Myshadows Morning News.** *M.* Seal Point Himalayan-Persian.
13. **Jovan Rayna of Gyzndolz.** *F.* Black Persian.
14. **Mellowmews Lord Murphy of Jensen.** *M.* Ruddy Abyssinian.
15. **Dabru Blue Thunder of Blue Pride.** *M.* Russian Blue.